DEPENDENT ORIGINATION

A Layperson's Perspective

By

Ron Wijewantha

Edited by
A.G.S.Kariyawasam

Buddhist Publication Society
Kandy * Sri Lanka

Buddhist Publication Society
P.O. Box 61
54, Sangharaja Mawatha
Kandy, Sri Lanka

National Library of Sri Lanka -
Cataloguing-in-Publication Data

Wijewantha, Ron
Paticcasamuppada: dependent origination:
the road to liberation / Ron Wijewantha; ed
by A.G.S. Kariyawasam - Kandy : Buddhist
Publication Society, 2002 - 130 p.; c.m.
ISBN 955-24-0237-9
i. 294.34 DDC 2   ii. title
iii. Kariyawasam, A.G.S. ed.
1. Buddhism

ISBN 955-24-0237-9

Printed in Sri Lanka by
M.D. Gunasana and Co. Ltd.,
Colombo, Sri Lanka.

THE WHEEL PUBLICATION No. 450/452

Table of Contents

To

Maha Thera Bhikkhu Bodhi PhD.,

&

Maha Thera M. Seelawimala MA.,

With Respect and Admiration

ACKNOWLEDGMENTS

This book would not have been possible but for the encouragement I received from many people.

Madawala Seelawimala Mahathera and Bhikkhu Bodhi Mahathera have been my primary sources of inspiration. The former, my mentor for encouraging me and providing me with access to his library and his deep knowledge of the suttas, and the latter by his continuing authorship of a vast number of tracts explaining important suttas in simple yet elegant and lucid language. To both of them I have much pleasure in dedicating this book.

My friend Sondra Jewel as well as Henepola Gunaratana Nayaka Thera (author of several books on meditation), Madawela Seelawimala Mahathera, and Prof Lily de Silva read through the script critically and pointed out inconsistencies and inaccuracies, and suggested appropriate corrections.

My three daughters, their spouses and my three grandsons helped me in many ways. So did Dr Udeni Balasuriya and Dr Jatal Mannapperuma. It is not possible to state in words how much I owe Sita, my dearest wife of nearly fifty years. She has given me much-needed encouragement at all times, and constantly prodded me to stay on track.

Mr A.G.S.Kariyawasam has enriched this presentation with careful editing.

Many people in the Sacramento-Davis-Woodland area participated in my *vipassanā* meditation programmes over the last seven years, and many others participated in the Friday meditation and discussion group at the West Sacramento Buddhist Temple. Their enthusiasm, comments and questions have in many ways acted as a catalyst to my comprehending many aspects of the Dhamma, which otherwise I had previously taken for granted.

This book is written in memory of my dear departed parents Arthur and Gertrude and our dear son Ajith. May their journey through *saṁsāra* be short and free of difficulties and dangers.

It is with much pleasure that I offer all those mentioned above my grateful thanks and the merit accruing from the writing of this book:

"The Gift of the Dhamma, exceeds all other gifts".

California, October 2002.
Ron W.

AUTHOR'S PREFACE

In this presentation, we shall proceed on a voyage of discovery. We shall first briefly discuss the fundamental philosophy and doctrine of the Buddha, and then try to discover ourselves. We shall see what we are really made of at the fundamental level. We shall then observe how the mind and body work in close association, and the pre-eminent position occupied by the mind in this process. Next we shall address the issue of our moral weaknesses and strengths, and discover how mindfulness can make us better members of society.

We shall discover the message underlying the doctrine of Dependent Origination or *Paṭiccasamuppāda* and then use such information as a tool to understanding that everything in this world is insubstantial, conditioned and that what we had understood as a permanent "I" is a mental illusion, and that everything in the universe is subject to decay, impermanence and suffering. This realization at the experiential level will encourage us to follow the Noble Eightfold Path as a way to escape from the *samsaric* round of births, deaths and rebirths.

At the end of each chapter, there will be some footnotes giving references to the texts as well as Pali words as they first appear in the texts. References to the Buddha's own words as quoted from the suttas have also been incorporated into the footnotes.

To make some of the explanations easily comprehensible, I have occasionally used examples from various scientific disciplines. Undoubtedly these could be replaced by even better examples as we continue expanding our scientific frontiers. Hopefully my attempts will suffice for the present.

Let us only keep in mind the timelessness of the Buddha-word.

The few pages on *vipassanā* meditation were based on the meditation practices of groups of participants and myself. They are certainly not meant to replace well-recognized meditation masters or the many excellent books on the practice. They are only for temporary guidance until a suitable meditation master is found. Some books on meditation are listed at the end of the book. However, meditation teachers and books can help only up to a point. Ultimately it is the readers themselves who will have to do the work.

I make no claim to originality in what I have presented in this book. It is based on the discourses of the Buddha and the commentaries and essays thereon by various distinguished authors too numerous to enumerate. What is new is only the method of presentation which emphasizes the fact that escape from suffering and attainment of liberation is within our grasp, provided we make the attempt by comprehending the *dhamma* and gaining insight into the true nature of all conditioned phenomena through *vipassanā* meditation.

Finally, I take full responsibility for whatever omissions and errors there may be in the interpretation of the profound doctrine of Dependent Origination or *Paṭiccasamuppāda,* as well as in the rest of the presentation.

I wish you happy reading!

Ron W.

ABBREVIATIONS

D	:	Dīgha Nikāya
S	:	Samyutta Nikāya
M	:	Majjhima Nikāya
A	:	Anguttara Nikāya
Dh	:	Dhammapada
Sn	:	Suttanipāta

All PTS editions

Namo tassa bhagavato arahato sammāsambuddhassa

(Homage to Him, the Exalted, the Worthy, the Fully Enlightened One!)

Chapter I

PRELIMINARY

The *Paṭiccasamuppāda,*[1] also known as dependent origination and Causal Genesis, contains the central **doctrine** of the Buddha and complements His central **teaching** which is the Four Noble Truths[2]. It is acknowledged by all to be a teaching that continues to be a challenge to students of Buddhism in their attempts at understanding it. However, a mere intellectual understanding of dependent origination is not enough. The truth contained therein must be directly grasped, personally experienced and intuitively penetrated if we are to reap the maximum benefits from it. In the text which follows, the term *paṭiccasamuppāda* and dependent origination will be used interchangeably.

There is yet another reason why we need to understand and comprehend it experientially, for it is eventually a direct way to the penetration and understanding of impermanence or inconstancy, unsatisfactoriness or distress, and non-self or no-soul—*anicca, dukkha* and *anatta*. It is with this combined understanding that we can achieve liberation which is the extinction of suffering and freedom from rebirth.

In the contemporary scene with so much interest in Buddhism in the West, it is perhaps opportune to offer a simple and an easily understandable book containing the basic tenets of Buddhism, plus an explanation of dependent origination and a method by which this knowledge could be used to achieve liberation. What is not called for is any previous knowledge of Buddhism. All that is required is an open, unprejudiced mind. This book will, therefore, lead the reader through an understanding of the doctrine of dependent origination to its intimate relationship with the Four Noble Truths and finally to insight into our very own selves through *vipassanā*[3] meditation.

This book is not meant for those who have a deep knowledge of the *Dhamma,*[4] whether they are erudite scholars or senior members of the *Saṅgha*[5] endowed with vast knowledge of this and other doctrines of the Buddha. It is meant only for those who are presently engaged in or intend to be *vipassanā* meditators, possessing perhaps only a modicum of knowledge of the Dhamma, but, having the enthusiasm to use whatever relevant information they acquire as an aid on their journey towards final liberation.

Nevertheless, a short list of books on dependent origination is provided at the end of the text for those whose interest in it is philosophical, intellectual or academic.

The Buddha

The Buddha to-be was born over 2500 years ago into the Sakyan Clan in a small state bordering India, which nestled in the Himalayan foothills in what we now call Nepal. He was heir to the Sakyan throne and lived a life of luxury in the capital city, Kapilavastu.

When he reached his late twenties, shielded by his father from life's natural phenomena of birth, decay, illness and death, the prince was suddenly exposed to four eye-opening experiences: A man weakened with age, a man decimated by sickness, decay and decrepitude, a corpse being carried on the shoulders of grieving relatives for cremation and an ascetic moving with measured step, downcast eyes and a serene countenance.

The prince thereafter became increasingly introspective and thoughts such as the following began to stir within him with increasing intensity: "Youth, the prime of life, ends in old age and man's senses fail him at a time when they are most needed. The hale and hearty lose their vigour and health when disease creeps in. Finally death comes perhaps suddenly and unexpectedly, and puts an end to this brief span of life. Surely there must be an escape from this unsatisfactoriness, from ageing and death.[6]

"Suppose that, being myself subject to ageing, sickness and death, to sorrow and defilement, I seek the unageing, unailing, deathless, sorrowless and undefiled state, the supreme security from bondage, Nibbāna"[7].

Accordingly, at the age of 29, on the day of the birth of his only child Rāhula, he left his kingdom, from home to homelessness, discarding the enchantment of the royal life, rejecting the joys and pleasures that most young people yearn for. He cut off his long hair with his sword, set aside his royal robes and putting on an ascetic's garb, retreated into sylvan solitude to seek a solution to those problems of life that had deeply stirred his mind - a solution, an answer to the riddle of life. A true, real and practical way out of unsatisfactoriness and suffering, leading to enlightenment[8] and Nibbāna.[9]

He then spent six long years in experimentation, self-mortification, reflection, contemplation and meditation. Although these efforts were ultimately helpful in formulating his doctrines in due course, they did not directly help in his quest for enlightenment and liberation. The *bodhisatta* (the name given to an aspirant before he attains enlightenment) now thought 'is there another way for me to strive towards enlightenment?'

And he brought to mind an incident which took place just a short while back when a team of itinerant musicians and dancing girls had passed through the grove where he was in meditation. Unaware of his presence, they had played their instruments and one of the dancing girls had shouted out to the lute-player and asked him to play a tune, but warned him not to tune his lute too low nor too high. For, she said: 'good music can be made only when the lute is tuned to the correct pitch between these two extremes'. And here a lesson could be learnt, he thought.

"Self-mortification and self-indulgence are two extremes to be avoided."[10]

As a result, he decided then and there to adopt this middle way, one which balanced care of the body with sufficient time available for contemplation and deep investigation. One day when his physical strength had returned, he approached a lovely spot in Uruvelā by the banks of the river Neranjarā. There he prepared, underneath a Ficus tree (later to be called the Bodhi Tree - *ficus religiosa*), a seat of newly cut *kusa*-grass donated by a grass-cutter. He then sat on it cross-legged, making a firm resolution that he would not rise up until he had won the goal of liberation, Nibbāna.

As night descended he entered into deeper and deeper stages of meditation until his mind was perfectly calm and composed. In the first watch of the night there unfolded before his inner vision his experiences in many past births, extending over many cosmic eons; in the middle watch of the night he developed the "divine eye" by which he could see beings passing away and taking rebirth in accordance with their *kamma*[11] and in the last watch he directed his concentration and focused his mind to the penetration of the deeper truths of existence. Through this he gained insight into the *paṭiccasamuppāda* or the chain of conditioned existence encompassing the most basic laws of reality and thereby removed from his mind even the subtlest veil of ignorance. When dawn broke, He had achieved what he had been striving for. He had "awakened" from ignorance. He had reached Enlightenment. He was a Buddha who had in this very life attained the Deathless, the Unconditioned which is Nibbāna.[12]

He was now ready to share his discoveries, his Dhamma, with one and all. Towards this end, he formulated his discoveries into four simple laws, which he called the Four Noble Truths, truths which, when fully and properly comprehended, ennobled the practitioner by his realizing the goal of Nibbāna. (Hence the word 'Noble' which precedes the word 'Truths').

The Four Noble Truths

1. Dukkha - Suffering or unsatisfactoriness or distress
2. Dukkha-samudaya - The origin of suffering
3. Dukkha-nirodha (Nibbāna) - The cessation of suffering and

4. Dukkha- nirodha- gaminī- paṭipadā – The way to the end
of unsatisfactoriness, which is the Noble Eightfold Path.

Thereafter, in many a sermon during his fortyfive-year
ministry, he gave prominence to the Four Noble Truths.

"It is because we have not understood, not penetrated the
Four Noble Truths that we have wandered so long in this
beginingless *saṁsāra*[13]. Those who fully penetrate the truths
are freed from *saṁsāra*[13] (D.ii, 90).

To penetrate and comprehend these Four Noble Truths
we need more information about them.

Suffering *(dukkha)*. *Dukkha* is the first Noble Truth.
Although *dukkha* has often been translated as 'suffering', the
words that encapsulate its meaning best are: unsatisfactoriness,
distress or discomfort. The Buddha says that there is
unsatisfactoriness in the world.

The 'world' in this case refers to us, the living beings, for
the Buddha has often said that this fathom-long body of ours
is the world. (A fathom in the ancient world was the distance
from the tip of the middle finger of one outstretched hand to
the tip of the middle finger on the other outstretched hand. -
this incidentally is the height of that person. – Mariners
consider a fathom as 6 feet in length).

The Buddha would often use the word 'world' when
referring to what we recognize to be a person, as can be seen
in the following incident where a novice monk appears
confused and blurts out:

Novice monk: "The world, the world *(loka)*" it is said.
"To what extent does the word 'world' apply"?

The Buddha : "It disintegrates *(lujjati)* and therefore it is
called the "world". Now, what disintegrates? The eye

disintegrates. So also for ear, nose, tongue, body, consciousness and their corresponding sense data... It disintegrates, therefore it is called the 'world'". (S.xxxv.82).

All sentient beings live a life full of suffering, both physical and mental, and it is the mental aspect which can bring us most harm. For, in addition to our becoming emotionally upset when things go wrong, we can also, by reacting negatively, accumulate a lot of negative *kamma*.

Origin of Suffering *(dukkha-samudaya)* is the second Noble Truth. The origin of suffering is craving rooted in ignorance. Craving *(taṇhā)* can have a deeper meaning too. It is a combination of greed and selfishness rolled into one. When craving becomes intense it changes to clinging, *(upādāna)*. Craving can be of various types. Sensual craving *(kāma-taṇhā)*, craving for life *(bhava-taṇhā)* and even craving for the extinction of life *(vibhava-taṇhā)*.

Cessation of suffering *(dukkha-nirodha)* **or Nibbāna:** Nibbāna is the third Noble Truth. It is the unconditioned, the undefinable, the ultimate truth, the steady state, the inactivated state where there is no more conditioning. It is timeless, without a past and without a future, the changeless state free from all causation, the transcendental condition.

The fourth Noble Truth is the path leading to the end of suffering *(dukkha-nirodha-gāminī paṭipadā)*. It is the path, the way to the end of unsatisfactoriness. It is called the Noble Eightfold Path, which if followed will lead to Nibbāna. This path is beautifully summarized by the Buddha when answering a deity[14]: "Tangled within, tangled without, mankind is entangled in a tangle. I ask this question, Gotama: Who disentangles this tangle?" asked a deity.

"When the wise man established in virtue (*sīla*) develops concentration (*samādhi*) and wisdom (*paññā*), then as a *bhikkhu* ardent and prudent, he disentangles this tangle" replied the Buddha. (S.i.13).

As it can be seen from the above, the Buddha shows that these eight steps of the Path can be arranged within three groups. Virtue or morality (*sīla*), concentration (*samādhi)* and wisdom *(paññā).*

The eight factors of the Noble Eightfold Path are:

Skilful Understanding ⎫
Skilful Thought   ⎬   wisdom or *paññā* group
                                    ⎭

Skilful Speech   ⎫
Skilful Action   ⎬   virtue/morality or *sīla* group
Skilful Livelihood   ⎭

Skilful Effort   ⎫
Skilful Mindfulness   ⎬   concentration or *samādhi* group
                                       ⎭

This eight-fold path is called the Middle Path as it avoids the two extremes of self-indulgence and self-mortification. It must be borne in mind that, although as a training programme one is expected to graduate from virtue/morality to concentration and then to wisdom, in actual practice they overlap or they are interdependent and inter-related, and the further we progress, the more interrelated they appear to be.

'Concentration (meditation), O Monks, supported by virtue brings much fruit, brings much advantage. Wisdom supported by concentration brings much fruit, much advantage. The mind supported by wisdom (right understanding) is wholly and entirely freed from the intoxication of sense desires, from becoming, wrong views and ignorance' (D.16).

It is useful at this stage to briefly explain the eight factors that make up the Noble Eightfold Path. We shall start with morality/virtue (*sīla*).

Morality or *sīla* group

Skilful Speech: Along with skilful speech we must also look at non-skilful speech such as slander, gossip, idle chatter, false and harsh speech. Once we remove these impurities, we are left with skilful speech.

Skilful physical action: Non-skilful physical action is when we hurt, wound or kill sentient beings. So also if we steal, borrow with no intention of returning, participates in sexual misconduct and use intoxicants. What will then remain is purity of action. Intoxicants include, in the broader sense, various hallucinating drugs and any substance which causes people to lose their sense of proportion or their sense of values. A person could in fact become unskilful when intoxicated with power because of the position the person holds.

Skilful livelihood: It is important that we should abstain from earning a living by means which bring harm to others, such as dealing in intoxicants, fire-arms, running gambling dens, owning shares in casinos, prostitution and so on.

A good criterion for what is unskilful livelihood is motivation. If one's motivation is impure, then that living is unskilful. For example, if a practising physician were to wish that people in his community be frequently struck down by epidemics, necessitating medical intervention so that he could make more money, then his motivation is bad. Similarly, if a merchant were to wish for scarcities and non-availability of essential food items so that he could raise the price of his goods arbitrarily, then his motivation too is bad, and his livelihood is unskilful.

How can both these persons conform to skilful livelihood? One suggestion is that both of them change their attitudes and develop *mettā* or universal kindness first towards themselves and then towards the rest of the members of the community. Another is to set aside, in the case of the physician, perhaps a half day each week for treatment of disadvantaged members of the community and, in the case of the merchant, a certain percentage of his monthly profits for charity or to subsidize purchases made by disadvantaged persons in the neighbourhood.

2. The concentration or *samādhi* group

The first step is **skilful effort**. In our daily life, we are frequently told to take physical exercise when we feel weak. It is the same with the mind. While it is yet untamed, it requires plenty of good exercise. We could therefore do a number of things: First we must look at the mind and see whether it has any defilements.

i. If we see any defilement, (here we have to be honest

with ourselves about it) we need to get rid of them.

ii. If there are no visible defilements, then we need to guard the sense-doors comprising the eyes, ears, nose, tongue, body and mind (thoughts).

iii. If we see virtues, try to retain and multiply them.

vi. If we see no good qualities, develop and cultivate them by keeping the sense-doors open, and by means of *vipassanā* meditation (see chapter 6).

Some of the advice, which the Buddha gave young novice Rāhula, his erstwhile son, on the above is relevant here. He said:

"Develop the meditation on *mettā* (loving-kindness) Rāhula, for, Rāhula, by developing *mettā*, ill-will is abandoned.

"Develop the meditation on *karuṇā* (compassion), Rāhula, for, Rāhula, by developing compassion, cruelty is abandoned.

"Develop the meditation on *muditā* (appreciative joy), Rāhula, for, Rāhula, by developing *muditā*, aversion is abandoned.

"Develop the meditation on *upekkhā* (equanimity), Rāhula, for, Rāhula, by developing equanimity, Rāhula, hatred is abandoned.

"Develop the meditation on *asubha* (impurity), Rāhula. for, Rāhula, by meditating on impurity, lust is abandoned.

"Develop the meditation on *anicca* (impermanence)

Rāhula, for, Rāhula, by meditating on impermanence,
pride of self is abandoned" (M.61).

The next is **skilful mindfulness.** This means present
awareness, awareness of the present moment, not the moment
before or the moment to come. This is what we do when we
focus on the breath during *vipassanā* meditation. Awareness
of everything happening as it is. Observing the truth as it is,
nature as it is, and all sensations from the grossest to the
most subtle. It is seeing reality, not imagination, and when
observing, not reacting to gross sensations, but just observing
without identifying any of them as belonging to us.

Skilful concentration is the third step in this group. During
vipassanā meditation, we learn from experience that we can
concentrate on both good and bad thoughts! It is unskilful
when we concentrate on the past or on the future. These
thoughts are counter-productive. They lead to illusions,
delusions and confusion. It is skilful concentration that purifies
the mind, freeing it from aversion and attachment. It is
continuous awareness of reality within the framework of the
body.

Wisdom or *paññā* group

What is wisdom (*paññā*)? Before discussing this, let us keep
in mind that the morality (*sīla*) group comprises the first three
steps on our journey along the path to liberation. It also helps
us to avoid negative actions, which harm both others and
ourselves.

Concentration *(samādhi)* group

Equally important is the second group of three steps: the concentration *(samādhi)* group, which helps to develop our mastery over the mind and lays the foundation for developing *paññā* or wisdom. It is wisdom *(paññā)* that is absolutely necessary to attain the liberation of Nibbāna.

With the help of the first two groups, we can remove some impurities on the surface of the mind. However, while doing so, instead of getting rid of gross negativities, we actually push most of them into the unconscious or deeper level of the mind where they are called *anusaya*. It is here that they accumulate like dormant volcanoes, ready to erupt when given the proper time and circumstance. These volcanoes are the old stock of defilements called 'klesha'. It is by developing wisdom and insight[15] that we can ultimately remove even the last traces of impurities from the mind. This allows us to stop generating negative *kamma*.

Wisdom or paññā is of three types called *sutamaya-paññā*, *cintāmaya-paññā* and *bhāvanāmaya-paññā*. They are progressive steps:

Sutamaya-paññā is wisdom from reading appropriate texts, listening to discourses and participating in discussions. But this is other people's learning! We therefore have to be careful that we do not accept everything we hear or read, for we can become conditioned and turn to blind faith. The Buddha has advised against blind faith.

Advising the Kālāma people He said. "... Now look you Kālāmas, do not be led by reports, or tradition, or hearsay.

Be not be led by the authority of religious texts, nor by mere
logic or inference, nor by considering appearances, nor by
the delight of speculative opinions, nor by seeming
possibilities, nor by the idea: 'this is our teacher'. But, O
Kālāmas, when you know for yourselves that certain things
are unwholesome and wrong and bad, then give them up...And
when you know yourselves that certain things are wholesome
and good, then accept them and follow them"(A. Vol, 1.p189).

Cintāmaya-paññā is what we conclude by analysis,
contemplation and reflection on what we have heard. It is
wisdom acquired through one's own thinking but based on
what one had heard. And here it is appropriate also to keep
in mind the four reliances:

> "Do not rely on individuals, rely on the teachings
> Do not rely on the words, rely on the meanings
> Do not rely on the adapted meanings, rely on the
>   ultimate meanings
> Do not rely on intellectual knowledge, rely on
>   wisdom" [16].

The third is *bhaāvanāmaya-paññā*. This is insight or
experiential wisdom that can lead us to liberation, to Nibbāna.
However, we should remember that the first two have played,
and will always continue to play a very important role, for it
is these two concepts that directed us to the third. The three
factors are like a three-legged stool. Take away one leg and
the stool will collapse. It is wisdom through meditation that
helps us to loosen all the knots that we have been tying every
day of our lives, and it helps us to eradicate all impurities,

particularly the three root causes of our wandering in *saṁsāra* - *lobha, dosa,* and *moha* (greed, hatred and delusion) and thus to open our minds to direct wisdom.

Let us look deeper into the two specific steps of the Path within the Wisdom group.

The first is **skilful thought**. Our thought processes are most of the time coloured by illusions, delusions, confusion and wrong thoughts. This is called *ayoniso manasikāra.* We need to change it to thinking in the proper way called *yoniso manasikāra.* We slowly begin to get an inkling of the truth by removing defilements first at the surface level of the mind. By practising *vipassanā* meditation we start noticing bad and impure thoughts as they arise and surface. But, by simply observing them with equanimity and letting them go, they can be eradicated. Now our thought patterns change to thinking in the proper way and we are ready to go to the final step of the path, namely skilful understanding.

Skilful understanding: Proper thoughts now start appearing. This is possible because we can now look deeper into the unconscious layers of the mind. By thinking in the proper way, we start seeing reality as it is, without illusions, delusions and confusion. We see nature with its true characteristics, as it really is. We are now able to progress through the three types of wisdom discussed above.

We see the 'bigger-picture' now: that there is no real 'I', but merely processes which come to be and die, that all beings are inter-connected and subject to conditionality, and that the underlying theme is the need for harmony, kindness, and compassion if one is to progress to wisdom and ultimately take the first transcendental[17] step to Nibbāna.

We conclude the discussion of the Path with the Buddha's own words:

> From skilful understanding proceeds purity of thought
> From skilful thought proceeds purity of speech
> From skilful speech proceeds purity of action
> From skilful action proceeds purity of livelihood
> From skilful livelihood proceeds purity of effort
> From skilful effort proceeds purity of awareness
> From skilful awareness proceeds purity of concentration
> From skilful concentration proceeds purity of wisdom
> From skilful wisdom proceeds liberation.

Chapter II

Prerequisites to Understanding
the Paticcasamuppāda

The Buddha, while unequivocally stating that the way to liberation is to follow the Noble Eightfold Path, has also provided us with complementary pathways to help us reach this same goal.

Thus on a certain occasion when visiting the Kuru[1] people He expounded the Mahā Satipaṭṭhāna Sutta[2]. In the introduction itself he has said, "This is the only way *(ekāyano maggo)* for the purification of beings, for the surmounting of sorrow and lamentation, for the abandoning of pain and grief, for reaching the Right Path and realizing Nibbāna, that is the setting up of the Four-fold Mindfulness" (M.10).

On another occasion He has stated, "He who sees dependent origination sees the Dhamma, He who sees the Dhamma sees the dependent origination" (M.28).

The purpose of this book is to explore the latter, viz., dependent origination.

We cannot liberate ourselves from suffering *(dukkha)* merely by the intellectual understanding of this profound doctrine. On the contrary, we shall see as we proceed that we can truly understand it only by total immersion in this doctrine. This understanding is progressively structured. The first level of knowledge is by reading, listening and studying the suttas[3] and is called *sutamaya-paññā*. This is followed by analytical knowledge known as *cintāmaya-paññā*. We can then carry it to the final level of knowledge, which is experiential wisdom known as *bhāvanāmaya-paññā* and reached only by insight (*vipassanā*) meditation. It is at this stage that we achieve wisdom and insight into the interconnectedness of all phenomena, of their impermanence and distress, leading finally to our realization of the Truth. Thus, by comprehending experientially this most difficult doctrine, the gateway to at least the first stage of liberation, that of Stream-winner (*sotāpanna*), will be opened to us.

It is essential that those who start on this journey equip themselves first with a factual working knowledge of the Dhamma so that the journey of discovery becomes easier. Such 'knowledge' will be of immense benefit in understanding each of the links or factors comprising the *paṭiccasamuppāda*..

The subjects, which we shall presently study, are:

1. *Saṁsāra.*
2. Nibbāna.
3. The 5 Aggregates comprising mind and matter.
4. *Kamma* and Rebecoming (Rebirth).
5. The three universal characteristics of all conditioned things, – impermanence (*anicca*), suffering (*dukkha*) and non-self (*anatta*).

6. Conditionality

7. The four steps to liberation which are that of stream-winner(*sotāpanna*), once-returner (*sakadāgāmi*), non-returner (*anāgami*) and finally the fully liberated person, the *arahat*.

Saṁsāra

Saṁsāra is the process of birth and death without beginning. *Saṁsāra* means 'the round of rebirth' or more literally 'the wandering around' continuously. According to classical terminology, it could be said that *saṁsāra* extends over manifold worlds (*loka*) and involves rebirth into various planes of existence, based on one's *kamma*. The Buddha has said: "Bhikkhus, this *saṁsāra* is without conceivable beginning. No first point is discerned of beings roaming and wandering (in *saṁsāra*), bonded by ignorance and fettered by craving..." (S. II, 178, 182). Our aim should therefore be to terminate this cycle of birth, death and rebirth

In Buddhist texts, the word used to denote the cosmos or universe is 'loka'. Its uses are as numerous as the English word 'world'. The early Buddhist texts do not state that the major world-systems are all there in the universe. The question of whether the world is finite or infinite is left unanswered. The standpoint of early Buddhism was to state that the universe was "without a known beginning" and that it is 'conditioned'.

As for the end, this will occur only at the end of an epoch or an aeon, called *kappa*. Several similes are given to illustrate what an immensely long period an aeon is. One such passage reads as follows: 'Suppose there was a city of iron walls one *yojana* in length, one in width and one high, filled with mustard seeds, from which a man were to take out at the end of every hundred years a mustard seed. That pile of mustard seeds would in this way be sooner done away with than an aeon, so very long is an aeon. And of aeons thus long, more than one has passed, more than a hundred, more than a thousand, more than a hundred thousand' (S.11.182).

Nibbāna (Sansk: Nirvāṇa)

We have discussed Buddhist cosmology briefly in order to understand *saṁsāra* better, – the unbroken and continuing process of rebirth which can occur in any plane of existence in the cosmos, depending on one's performance. All such rebirths, it is important to note, are "conditioned".

There is on the other hand a blissful state of complete spiritual freedom. This is the state of Nibbāna. It is an unconditioned state, a peaceful state, and a state totally free of greed, aversion and delusion. It is a state, which once reached, prevents the person from returning to the round of *saṁsāra*.

But to arrive at this state of Nibbāna, one has to follow a path of purification. Only a supremely enlightened being, namely a Buddha, can show such a path to us. Our aim should be to realize the bliss of Nibbāna by following his instructions. These instructions were laid down by him in his very first discourse, and are contained in the Fourth Noble Truth as the Noble Eightfold Path.

It is a path, which leads to emancipation and complete freedom from the conditioned. The Buddha assures us that by following this path with mindfulness, wisdom and proper application Nibbāna can be realized here and now.

The Five Aggregates *

At the conventional level we know that we have a body and a mind, but at the supra-mundane or transcendental level[4] we can go deeper and redefine them. The Buddha found that by penetratingly examining his own nature, he could comprehend the reality within himself.

He realized that every sentient being is a composite of five processes, which he called aggregates (*khandha*) four of which are mental, which He called *nāma*, and the other physical, called *rūpa*. He found that mentality and materiality always work in unison. There is mutual interaction between the physical base and mental activity. They are interconnected and have a cause and effect relationship. However, at the same time the Buddha has emphasized that it is the mind that is foremost:

> 'Mind is the forerunner of all phenomena.
> Mind is chief, everything is mind-made.
> If one speaks or acts with an impure mind,
> Suffering follows one, as the cartwheels
> follow the foot of the draught-animal.'

... If one speaks or acts with a pure mind,
 ... Happiness follows one as a shadow that never leaves.
(Dh 1-2).

What is this thing known as the **Mind** or *nāma*? The Buddha has observed that the four aggregates comprising the mind were fundamentally nothing but four processes in constant interaction with one another. They are:

Sensation or feeling *(vedanā)*

Perception, sense-impressions and concepts *(saññā)*

Reaction/ mental formations, cognative activities *(saṅkhāra)*

Consciousness *(viññāṇa)*

The first three of the aforementioned mental processes are considered as concomitants or adjuncts of the fourth, consciousness, which is defined as the primary factor of mental life. To picture the way these four processes interact and work together, we have to look at familiar examples. Consider our own endocrine system. It is a group of specialized organs and body tissues that produce, store and secrete chemical substances known as hormones. As the body's chemical messengers, hormones transfer information and instructions from one set of cells to another. Because of the hormones they produce, endocrine organs have a great deal of influence over the body.

These organs are sometimes called ductless glands because they have no ducts connecting them to specific body parts. The hormones they secrete are released directly into the bloodstream. The primary glands that make up the human endocrine system are the hypothalamus, pituitary, parathyroid, adrenal, pineal and the reproductive glands. The pancreas, an organ often associated with the digestive system, is also considered part of the endocrine system.

The hypothalamus, found deep within the brain, directly controls the pituitary gland. It is often described as the coordinator or the conductor of the endocrine system. When information reaching the brain indicates that changes are needed somewhere in the body, nerve cells in the hypothalamus secrete chemicals that either stimulate or suppress hormone secretions from the pituitary gland. Acting as liaison between the brain and the pituitary gland, the hypothalamus is the primary link between the endocrine and the nervous systems.

Now consider a musical sextet or a string quartet. Here too, the individual musicians have to be coordinated under a single leader, a conductor or lead-player in order to produce harmonious music. As in these examples, our mind requires a lead-player, and it is consciousness which plays this part. It is also consciousness which ensures the continuity of the individual through the duration of a single life. When a person is in an inactive state, like when he is sleeping or unconscious, this life-continuum consciousness lies dormant in what is called a *bhavaṅga* state. But when a sense organ makes contact (*phassa*) with a sense object, then the appropriate sense consciousness is activated as shown below, producing the desired effect:

contact	*phassa*
consciousness	*viññāṇa*
sensation	*vedanā*
perception	*saññā*
conceiving	*vitakka*
differentiation	*papañca*
reaction	*saṅkhāra*

One mind-moment

It will be noted from the above that in addition to the functioning of the four aggregates comprising the mind, two other activities of thought-perception and differentiation take place immediately after perception and before reaction or mental formation(*saṅkhāra*). In the Madhupiṇḍika sutta (M. 18), the complete process is described as follows: "...Dependent on the eye and forms, eye-consciousness arises. The meeting of the three is contact. With contact as a condition there is feeling. What one feels, that one perceives. What one perceives, that one thinks about. What one thinks about, that one mentally proliferates. What one has mentally proliferated as the source, perceptions and notions tinged by mental proliferation beset a man with respect to past, future and present forms cognizable through the eye. ..."

One mind-moment takes only a nano-second and is immediately followed by another and still another. At a maximum, seventeen mind-moments are needed for a single thought process to be completed. It is only after numerous mind-moments that *saṅkhāras* or mental formations result in fruition as a reaction. Hence it would not be incorrect to say that there is always consciousness to monitor everything that is happening, while triggering the other three aggregates to produce the desired effect. Thus, from the moment a person is born upto his last breath or mind-moment, these four processes occur continuously.

Perhaps we can better understand how the four aggregates of the mind work by means of a practical example. Suppose a man opens his front door, looks outside and sees an object moving in his direction.

    i. He is first aware in a general way of an approaching object. This is consciousness (*viññāna).*

    ii. He then, taking past experiences of the approaching

person into consideration, will either like or dislike the person. But if that person is unknown to him, he will remain neutral about liking or disliking. This is sensation (*vedanā*).

iii. He then recognizes the object/subject (by instantaneously comparing it against previous experiences). This is perception (*saññā*).

iv. Immediately thereafter, he will react (*cetanā*) with either pleasure or displeasure, or with no reaction (indifference), which will be followed by appropriate action. This is reaction (*saṅkhāra*).

Once this mind-moment is completed, it will be followed immediately by the next mind-moment and then another and so on. This is the pattern, which will be followed throughout life, except when one is asleep or rendered unconscious.

Hence, human experience can be considered to be a rapid sequence of mind-moments, which occur, in a fixed sequence of sensation, perception and reaction within the framework of consciousness. When the sensation phases become concentrated through this repetition of mind-moments, the reaction takes on a physical or a mental aspect. For instance, in the above example, the man may welcome the approaching person with kind words or, if he dislikes the person, the welcome could be a negative one. Finally, if the approaching person is a stranger, the welcome could be indifferent, such as 'may I help you?'

Citta: A single act of consciousness is called a *citta*. It is made up of many components. The principal factor in each *citta* is consciousness itself. Its function is the basic experiencing of the object and is itself given the name of the whole act viz, *citta*. Besides the aggregates themselves, there are the 'mental factors' such as emotions, which influence and give the *cittas* their distinctive character. The most important of these are the acts of consciousness (*cittas*) influenced by the mind when it is subject to the three defilements of greed, aversion and delusion, or to their opposites-non-greed, non-hate and non-delusion.

We have so far examined the way in which a thought-process operates by drawing on the *suttas*. Now, with this knowledge of how the mind works, we could give some more consideration by studying it in more detail, as explained in the Abhidhamma Piṭaka [5].

Abhidhamma and consciousness

Our consciousness receives signals all the time from within ourselves or from outside. The functional continuity of the consciousness of a person, as stated before, is ensured throughout that person's existence in this life from conception to death. This consciousness is called *bhavaṅga*. Whenever an object impinges on any sense-door, this *bhavaṅga*-consciousness is arrested, thus setting the stage for the cognitive and related processes such as perception, sensation and reaction to perform their respective functions. This is followed by volition (*saṅkhāra*). This is the stage, which is most important from an ethical point of view, since it is here that wholesome and unwholesome thoughts (*cetanā*), which are kammically effective, occur. This latter stage is given the name *javana* in the Abhidhamma.

It must be remembered that *bhavaṅga* supervenes

immediately after each cognitive process until the next cognitive process arises. "Arising and persisting at every moment during the passive phase of consciousness, the *bhavaṅga* flows on like a stream, without remaining static even for two consecutive moments."[6] The thought-processes that interrupt *bhavaṅga* -consciousness operate through the five sense doors (eyes, ears, nose, tongue, body and the mind).

Reaction/cognitive activities *(saṅkhāra)*

We have been examining *saṅkhāra*, the fourth aggregate, only as far as it denotes all those factors which accompany conscious volitional activities. There are, however, other definitions of *saṅkhāra* as well, but they are not directly relevant to understanding how the four aggregates of mentality work together. We need to remember that all four of the above psychological states, namely consciousness, perception, sensation and reaction are causally conditioned by various factors such as one's physical and social environment, by the physiological state of the body, our upbringing and previous experiences and so on. A gradual development of awareness *(sati)* by *vipassanā* meditation reveals to us these intricate relationships. "It also reveals the fact that the mind itself dissolves into a stream of *cittas* flashing in and out of being, moment to moment, coming from nowhere, yet continuing in sequence without pause"[7]

Lets us also remember that a human being's stream of consciousness has a conscious and an unconscious component. Our conscious mental activity gets into the 'unconscious' and accumulates in it, continuing to influence our conscious behaviour. In the unconscious state are the latent tendencies of the mind called the *anusayas*. These are the tendencies to satisfy our desires, our egoistic impulses or aggression, as well as the beliefs we cling to in the unconscious mind, such as doubt, wrong views, conceit, ignorance, arrogance and pride, just to name a few. These are factors, which need to be eradicated during our journey through *saṁsāra* .

Matter

Matter is all of the visible components that make up our body (*rūpa*), and at the ultimate level consists merely of four primary elements (*dhātu*).It is very difficult to define (*dhātu*) in modern terms and language, for they mean much more than what we know as elements of the periodic table and as 'particles' of current particle-science). For, in its original form, this word also conveys its characteristics.

They are:
Solid (*paṭhavi*) element.
Liquid *(āpo)* element.
Heat/fire *(tejo)* element.
Air/wind *(vāyo)* element.

We can understand them better by looking at their characteristics:
Solidity for the solid element.
Fluidity and cohesion for the liquid element.
Heat or caloricity for the heat element.
Movement for the wind/air element.
These four primary elements manifest themselves in the human

body in various permutations and combinations. But at the fundamental level they are sub-atomic particles in constant motion, arising and vanishing in unimaginably rapid succession. Ultimately matter is nothing but crystallization of energy, thus giving them an apparent false reality. Our skeletal structure has a preponderance of the solid element with small quantities of the others. Our circulatory and lymphatic systems are filled mainly with the fluid element, and the lungs and respiratory system are filled with the air element. Digestion and body warmth is performed by caloricity, and we can move about by a combination of the air and the fluid element.

In addition to the above, combinations of these primary elements are considered to have various types of secondary qualities such as colour, odour, taste and nutritive essence. The five aggregates, which we discussed above, cover the entire range of experience of a sentient being. Form covers all physical phenomena, both within one's body and without. The four remaining categories of mentality cover all mental events: feelings are characterized by pleasure, pain and neither pleasure nor pain, regardless of whether they are based on physical or mental sensations. Perception denotes the mental act of applying labels or names to physical or mental events. Mental formations cover the verbal and mental processes of concocting thoughts, questions, urges or intentions in the mind, while consciousness covers the act of consciousness at any of the six sense-doors: the eyes, ears, nose, tongue, body and intellect (mind).

It is by understanding the complex inter-relationships among these aggregates that one is led into the area of dependent origination. As one's understanding grows more sensitive, the point is driven home that all clinging to these phenomena should be abandoned.

Kamma and Rebirth

Let us take *kamma* first. It is the law that every action has some effect, some reaction.
We may have experienced and also realized that our actions affect the quality of our mind.

Each of our actions has an impact on our mind, and thus the quality of our mind has a direct influence on the quality of our life. The teaching of *kamma*, however, goes much deeper and gives a more thorough explanation of the whole process. Society is usually accustomed to measure the quality of actions predominantly by the impact they have on its surroundings. In the teaching of *kamma* we instead focus **on the effects our various actions have on ourselves.**

All actions performed through the three doors of body, speech and mind are *kamma*. More precisely, *kamma* is the volition, the intention – *cetanā*- behind the action. These *kammic* volitions have the inherent potential to bring about a corresponding type of result, a *kamma-vipāka*. Volitions have often been compared to seeds and the results they bring forth as the fruits. By *kamma* we mean the whole accumulated potential of all present and past volitions which have not yet produced their results.

The teaching of *kamma* is somewhat similar to the physical law of the preservation of matter and energy. *Kamma* might be considered an example of this law – the conservation of the positive and negative energy, which we generate, from the visible realm of matter into the more subtle dimensions of the mind. But we need to emphasize that while the physical law of action and reaction is mechanical, the law of *kamma* and *kamma-vipāka* rests on volition. For, each of our volitions leaves behind an imprint or dormant bud of energy in our minds, and when these *kammic* impulses ripen under suitable external conditions, they will bring forth some result.

Let us remember that mental processes or mental impulses are very significant. Think of the minds, which created the microchip or sent man to the moon. Truly the mind, as the Buddha said, is the forerunner of all actions. To impress on us the dynamics of *kamma*, let us bring to mind Newton's third law of motion; "For every action there is an equal and opposite reaction". The law of *kamma* is an impersonal energy dynamic, for when its effects are personalized or, in other words, experienced from the point of view of the personality, they are experienced as a reversal in that direction, **a coming back to the intender of the energy of his or her intention.** Those who can recollect playing with a 'Newton's cradle' will remember this vividly.[7]

In these examples the person who develops hatred for others experiences hatred from others. On the other hand, the person who develops love for others experiences love from others and so forth. In other words, **you receive from the world what you give to the world; what goes around comes around!**[7] However, we should always keep in mind that "although we used physical energy systems for ease of comprehension of *kamma* and *kamma-vipāka*, there is a distinct difference between the law of *kamma* and the law of physics. In the law of *kamma*, volition plays a critical role, and in the absence of greed, hatred and delusion, *kammic* energy is not generated. Further, with the attainment of Arahatship, no more *kammic* energy is generated for this very reason."[8]

We should remember that *kamma* is an immanent law, which governs the balancing of energy in our continuing existence. It is impersonal, yet a law, and the balancing of energy does not always occur within the span of a single lifetime. It is not a simple tit-for-tat kind of law. Therefore, without some knowledge of rebirth along with that of *kamma*, it is not possible for a person to understand the significance or the meaning of events in his or her own life.

Let us take a hypothetical example: Classmates of a student give him a derogatory nickname. He is quite unhappy and feels frustrated, and he does not understand that this experience is simply bringing to completion an impersonal process. The wrongs other people do to him are the direct result of one's own past actions, both in previous as well as in this present existence. But the student is not aware of this. Consequently, he could become, for example, angry or vengeful or depressed, or withdraw into sorrow to suffer in silence. Each of these responses creates *kamma*, another imbalance of energy, which in turn must be balanced sometime in the future. In this way, one *kammic* debt has been paid, so to speak. Unfortunately, without his realizing it, the student has created another *kammic* debt! (Incidentally, so have his tormentors).

Let us now look at the ethical side. Volitional actions may be 'morally wholesome', 'morally unwholesome', or morally neutral, and they may be actions which find expression in physical, verbal or mental behaviour.

The morally wholesome and unwholesome actions are said

to give rise to appropriate consequences: They may find expression in this life, the next, or in lives to come unless their potentialities are extinguished or they do not find an opportunity for fruition. **And the word *kamma* is used to denote volitional acts, which find expression in thoughts, words and deeds.**

If the volition, or intention behind an action is governed by the three unwholesome roots of greed, aversion or delusion (*loba, dosa, moha*), the ensuing *kamma* is unwholesome and will bring forth unsatisfactory, undesirable, unpleasant results. If our volition is governed by non-greed (generosity, selflessness), non-hatred (kindness, friendliness), and non-delusion (clear understanding, insight, wisdom), then the *kammic* force will be wholesome, bringing forth happiness and other desirable results.

It must be kept in mind that the teaching of Buddhism is not that of continuing to perform good *kamma* for the sake of rewards in continued *saṁsāric* existence. **On the contrary, it is the elimination of the effects of *kamma* by spiritual progress towards liberation.**

Re-becoming (rebirth)

What happens to a person when he/she dies? To the average person, the material and mental constituents of what we call a 'person' disintegrates - ashes to ashes dust to dust. But is that all? According to Buddhist understanding, the accumulated, and yet unused *kammic* energy gives impetus to the start of a new life. To put it in another way, the stream of mind-movements, driven forward by craving, conditions the initiation of a new series of consciousness, which continues in a new life form. Thus a new life comes into being.

Therefore, in the ultimate sense, our present life is a series of mind-moments rapidly rising and passing away, based on a single physical organism which too is subject to constant change. After death, this series of mind-moments of the consciousness continues, finding support in a new physical organism. The last moment of this life is followed by the first mind-moment at rebirth or re-becoming in a new existence. We may perhaps be uncertain as to whether there is a difference between re-birth and re-becoming. The word used to describe the evolution from existence to existence is re-becoming (*bhava*). Rebirth in this sense continues to take place until a person has spiritually evolved to the state of an Arahat.

One may then ask, 'is it I who is reborn, or is the being in the next existence someone else?' Before we answer this question, we need to understand more clearly 'who am I'? Perhaps the easiest way to comprehend this would be to look at your old photograph album. Compare the baby you were in your first year of life, then the child at 5 years of age, then at 10, next at 16, and so on to the present. Are they the same person or not? It is hard to say, and you may probably think that they, frankly, are not the same. Compare last month and now, and what about yesterday and today, then an hour ago? In fact you are not exactly the same person now as when you started to read this chapter, because from moment to moment we are not exactly the same, yet neither are we entirely different.

As another example, let us take a stream and a person bathing in it. The stream when he started to bathe and the stream when he finished bathing were not the same, for the water in the stream had constantly flowed by. In fact we would be also correct when we say that the person who bathed in the river is not the same as the one who left the stream for dry land. He too has changed considerably, with many biochemical and developmental changes having taken place during the interim period. Rebecoming means exactly the same thing. The being of the last existence and the being of the present life and the one due to arise in the future are not quite the same, but also not entirely different. According to Buddhism, 'he is neither the same nor another' (*na ca so, na ca añño*) when we give a strictly accurate description, although in common parlance we may say that he is the same person.

When we look at life, we see that no physical matter — what we call materiality —, from the dying body passes over to a new life. Neither does any part of the mind or aggregate of mentality (be it consciousness, or perception, or sensation) pass from the old life to the new. What connects the past existence with the present one is the same link that connects yesterday and today, and today and tomorrow. It is not a real 'I' but simply the sequence of cause and effect. It is important to see the relationship between *kamma* and rebirth in terms of the Dhamma, for it is *kamma* and rebirth which show us the principal laws of conditioned existence. These we shall study in the next chapter.

Kamma should never be understood as a kind of unchangeable fate. The most important and far-reaching result of our past *kamma* is re-becoming itself, re-becoming in a particular plane of existence. The plane of existence into which rebirth will occur is determined by the consciousness that arises just prior to death. In the case of human life, it refers to the place of birth, the country, the family and the parents. These crucial circumstances of our life occur in accordance with our past *kamma*.

Therefore, the only way to escape this wandering is by getting rid of as much defilements as possible. It is necessary for us to remove greed, hatred and delusion and develop the opposites of these, namely greedlessness, hatelessness or non-aversion and wisdom (non-delusion), respectively. These will eventually bring about a happy and an equanimous disposition conducive to morality, compassion, appreciative-joy and universal-kindness. With such positive mental qualities, it should be possible for us to proceed successfully along the Eightfold Path, ending finally in wisdom and liberation.

The arising of mind and body at conception and its continuity during the course of life is the result of our past volitions. More particularly, our mental and bodily features, our personality traits, propensity towards health or illness, beauty or ugliness, the quality of our sense faculties, our intelligence, popularity, social status and skills, – all these are fundamentally rooted in our past actions.

The three universal characteristics

According to the Dhamma, there are three universal characteristics common to all living and non-living things in the Universe.

They are:
- the characteristic of impermanence
- the characteristic of unsatisfactoriness
- the characteristic of selflessness

These three characteristics are always present in, or

connected with, existence and they tell us about the nature of existence.

As a result of understanding these three characteristics, we can learn to develop detachment. Once we understand and comprehend the fact that impermanence, unsatisfactoriness and non-self universally characterize all existence, we can eliminate our attachment to continued existence and enter the threshold of total liberation. This is the purpose of understanding these three characteristics: it removes attachment by identifying delusion and confusion — the misunderstanding that existence is permanent, pleasant and has something to do with the self.

This is why understanding the three characteristics is called wisdom.

i. **Impermanence (*Anicca*)**

The fact of impermanence should be obvious to anyone who looks objectively at life and the world in which we live. Everything is ever changing, subject to destruction, unstable, unreliable and constantly decaying. No matter how much we try to hold on to something, it is not the same as it was moments ago, — just like the person bathing in the stream that we examined earlier.

Another useful exercise is to closely observe and analyze in our minds the flame of a burning candle. We take note of the flame and we see five unique characteristics: the flame's arising, developing, continuing, flickering and dying out completely. This is what we should see as happening to all of us. For ours too is a cycle of impermanence of birth, growing up, being young and strong, ageing, decaying and finally passing away. Similarly, our mental states are also impermanent. At one moment we are happy, and at another sad. As infants, we hardly understand anything: as adults in the prime of life, we understand a great deal more and in our old age, we lose the power of our mental faculties and become like infants once again.

Human impermanence is well described by Shakespeare (1564-1616) in what he calls "the seven ages of man".

> ...At first the infant,
> Mewling and puking in the nurse's arms.
> And then the whining school- boy, with his satchel,
> And shining face, creeping like snail
> Unwillingly to school. And then the lover
> Sighing like furnace, with a woeful ballad
> Made to his mistress' eyebrow. Then a soldier,
> Full of strange oaths, and bearded like a pard,
> Jealous in honour, sudden and quick in quarrel,
> Seeking the bubble reputation
> Even in the cannon's mouth. And then the justice,
> In fair round belly with good capon lin'd,
> With eyes severe, and beard of formal cut,
> Full of wise saws and modern instances;
> And so he plays his part. The sixth age shifts
> Into the lean and slipper'd pantaloon,
> With spectacles on nose and pouch on side,
> His youthful hose well sav'd a world too wide
> For his shrunk shank; and his big manly voice,
> Turning again toward childish treble, pipes
> And whistles in his sound. Last scene of all,

That ends this strange eventful history,
In second childishness and mere oblivion,
Sans teeth, sans eyes, sans taste, sans everything.

From: As You Like It.

ii. Suffering or unsatisfactoriness (*Dukkha*)

The Buddha has said that whatever is impermanent is suffering
and whatever is impermanent and suffering is also non-self. I
need not elaborate on suffering or dissatisfaction as we have
dealt with this topic in chapter one. Briefly, we can say that
birth, decay, bodily and mental illness, death, sorrow,
lamentation, despair, separation from loved ones, non-
fulfillment of wishes, association with unpleasant people, living
under stressful circumstances and so on are suffering. We
could even say that dissatisfaction/unsatisfactoriness can take
place when worldly happiness comes and goes, and we crave
for more.

iii. Non-self (*Anatta*)

The third universal characteristic of existence is non-self,
impersonality or insubstantiality. This is one of the distinct
and unique features of the teachings of the Buddha. The
Buddhist doctrine of non-self denies a permanent entity or
soul which runs through different existences without change
of identity, while it does not deny the continuity of an evolving
consciousness — a stream of consciousness determining its
state of re-becoming in different forms of cosmic existence.

Briefly, we could perhaps understand that everything in
this world could be considered as self-less because we cannot

find a part in anything that can be called the self; nor can we tell our body not to get sick or to stop ageing. This so-called being is composed of just five components - body, feeling, perception, mental function and consciousness. None of these components can be called the self and even outside of these five factors there is no permanent 'self'. If just one of these components is removed, nothing remains. Since all things are changing all the time, including ourselves, there is no rationale for us to believe that there is a permanent self.

Before we leave these three subjects, let it be emphasized that the truth of impermanence must not only be accepted intellectually, but it must be experienced as a reality within ourselves during *vipassanā* meditation. By directly understanding impermanence, as well as non-self and unsatisfactoriness, we reach true insight, which leads to liberation. However, the Buddha realized and taught that full liberation comes only when the three fundamental evils of desire, hatred/aversion and delusion/confusion are extinguished. Then only one is freed from the bondage of 'self' with the destruction of ignorance.

Cause and effect

This too is a universal law. We can best understand it by way of examples. You see on TV that a poor child died in a car accident, and you send a modest cheque towards the burial fund. Cause and effect. Your grandson is mishandled on the playing field, and you scold the coach. Cause and effect. You learn and practise *vipassanā*, and you become a kinder and gentler person. Cause and effect. You see with surprise that people like you more. Cause and effect. Our neighbour shouts at another neighbour, and he retaliates in kind. Cause and effect.

Another example:
> "For want of a nail, the shoe was lost,
> For want of a shoe, the horse was lost,
> For want of a horse, the rider was lost,
> For want of the rider, the battle was lost."

Benjamin Franklin (1706-1790).

The best example of cause and effect can be found in the Four Noble Truths. Suffering, the first Noble Truth is the *effect* and craving the second Noble Truth is the *cause*. Wisdom, the fourth Noble Truth is the *cause* and the attainment of Nibbāna the Third Noble Truth is the *effect*. Thus every effect has a cause behind it

Conditionality

If we were to carefully examine phenomena in this world, we would see that everything is conditioned. Everything, both animate and inanimate, has arisen because of conditions and consequently is subject to impermanence.

We wish to have a home of our own. A new house. We find a developer and give him a plan for a house. He starts by first laying the foundation; then he brings all sorts of building materials to the site and constructs the house. We first see the skeletal framework of the building, and in stages the construction is completed. It is ready for occupation. When we move in, the house becomes a home. But if we dismantle the house, it gets reduced once again to its component parts. There is nothing permanent in it. The parts are impermanent.

So is the house. It came to be because of conditions. There is nothing substantial or permanent to be called a home, either.

In fact, this very universe or cosmos itself and everything in it are subject to conditionality. The ultimate truth about us is that we too are conditioned and subject to impermanence, suffering or unsatisfactoriness, and have no permanent self or 'I'. In these circumstances it is seen that we urgently need to be liberated from this suffering, this distress by realizing Nibbāna.

The Path to Liberation

The path to Nibbāna lies through the understanding of *saṁsāra*, and the state of mind that realizes Nibbāna is called liberation (*vimokkha*). The three contemplations leading to Nibbāna are called doors to liberation (*vimokkha-mukha*). If the door to liberation is the contemplation of impermanence, the signless liberation (*animitta-vimokkha*) arises. If it is the contemplation of suffering, the desireless/wishless liberation (*appaṇihita-vimokkha*) arises. If it is the contemplation of non-self, the voidness/emptiness liberation (*suññatā-vimokkha*) arises. The signless liberation focuses upon Nibbāna as devoid of the 'signs' determinative of a conditioned formation; the wishless liberation as freedom from the hankering of desire; and the emptiness liberation as devoid of a self or any kind of substantial identity. These three liberations signify precisely the contemplations of the three universal marks of the conditioned: impermanence, suffering, and selflessness.

In each case, the understanding of the conditioned and the realization of the unconditioned are found to lock together in direct connection, so that by penetrating the conditioned to its very bottom and most significant features, the aspirant passes through the door leading out of the conditioned to the supreme security of the unconditioned, which is Nibbāna. The breakthrough to the unconditioned comes in four stages called the four-supramundane paths. (next page). Each momentary path-experience eradicates a specific group of defilements ranked in degrees of coarseness and subtleness.

The Buddha saw humans as shackled by the chains of their own weaknesses. Destruction of all the shackles (fetters) will deliver one from the wheel of rebirths and it will be the end of the road leading to the blissful state of Nibbāna. There are in all ten such shackles or fetters. Destruction of all the shackles will deliver one from *samsāra* or round of renewed births and it will signal the end of the road leading to the blissful state of Nibbāna.

The ten fetters (*samyojana*)

1. Delusion of self or personality view
2. Doubt
3. Clinging to rules and believing in the efficacy of ceremonies and rituals
4. Sensuality
5. Ill will
6. Passion for earthly life
7. Desire for fine-material and immaterial existece
8. Conceit
9. Restlessnesss
10. Ignorance

The four supramundane paths of *sotāpanna, sakadāgāmi,*

anāgami and *arahat* cut off the above defilements in gradual stages. The path to Nibbāna consists of these four distinctive and progressive steps. Progression through each step indicates the eradication of a specific group of defilements ranked in degrees of coarseness and subtleness. With the first supramundane path the aspirant eradicates the first three of the above fetters. Thereby he/she becomes a 'stream-winner' (*sotāpanna*). This person is bound for deliverance in a maximum of seven more lives passed in the human or heavenly worlds. He will take rebirth among gods and men for a maximum of seven lives after which he will attain Nibbāna.

The second supramundane path attenuates fetters four and five to the point where they no longer arise frequently or obsessively. With such attainment the aspirant advances to the stage of a 'once-returner' (*sakadāgāmin)*, one who is due to return to the sense sphere world only one more time. By eliminating the two fetters of sense desires and aversion or ill will, the aspirant attains the supramundane state of 'non-returner' (*anāgami)*. The *anāgamin* is no longer bound to the sense sphere but is heading for rebirth in a pure divine abode (*suddhāvāsa*), where he/she will attain the final goal of Nibbāna.

The fourth of the supramundane paths cuts off the remaining five fetters. With such attainment the aspirant becomes an *arahat*, who has destroyed all the defilements and reached the state of perfection.

Chapter III

Paṭiccasamuppāda- The Doctrine

The Buddha followed the expounding of the Noble Eightfold Path with many other discourses, including those on *kamma* and rebirth and other related subjects to explain the nature of reality in a very encompassing way: in a way to make known the unsatisfactory and untenable predicament of all beings in *saṁsāra*. These dangers are very apparent when we consider the workings of the immanent law of *kamma*. In this way He made people to reflect on whether there was a reasoned and acceptable method for escape from this spiral of continuing existence. The Buddha, as a skilled teacher, adopted diverse styles of presentation of His Dhamma, depending on his audience - whether they were *devas*[1], *Saṅgha*, lay-disciples or non-believers. Because He laid stress on the importance of dependent origination[2], the Buddha in many later suttas (as recorded in the Tripitaka[3]) has explained the dependent origination in many ways.

Determining that the manner in which this profound doctrine would later be presented required the vast and unlimited intelligence that is possessed only by a Buddha, He needed a mode of presentation that was simple enough to memorize but not so simple as to distort the teaching. It should be kept in mind that over two thousand five hundred years ago, during the time of the Buddha, reading and writing was the exclusive right of the priestly Brahmin class. Hence an oral tradition had been developed to keep the Dhamma alive. He also needed words that would point to the immediate realization of awareness in the listener's mind. Finally, He needed a framework for the teaching as a whole so that those who wanted to pursue specific points could also keep track of the larger picture. The result was the *Paṭiccasamuppāda* —dependent origination, which was, of course, the Dhamma which the *bodhisatta* had penetrated and brought to fruition on the night of his awakening in becoming a Buddha, the Enlightened One.

Consequently, over the last 25 centuries the basic structure of this doctrine has come down to us undiluted and unchanged. Many have mastered it, and those of us who wish to do the same must follow the very same path used by our predecessors. At the outset, the Buddha warned people that it was a profound and difficult subject to comprehend. When Ānanda, His constant companion told him, "It is wonderful and marvelous, sir, how this dependent arising is so deep, yet to myself it seems as clear as clear can be". The Buddha replied, "Do not say so, Ānanda! Do not say so, Ānanda! This dependent arising, Ānanda, is deep and it appears deep." (Mahā Nidāna Sutta).

By announcing this doctrine as deep, He would stir the imagination and interest of the public, and people were bound to inquire why this discourse was so deep. Then they would, more often than not, want to study it. In a similar way, we too would like to understand and comprehend the Dhamma as contained within this discourse. For, in this age of advanced information technology, we now have many special facilities to help us and at the end of the rainbow is the proverbial pot of gold - Insight leading to liberation, and such release from suffering and the round of *samsāra* is the attainment of Nibbāna [4].

You will recollect that in chapter one we discussed what the Buddha discovered on the night of the day of His Enlightenment, namely the Truth of conditioned arising. He did this by reflecting on birth and death and the need to find the reason why one wanders in *samsāra* with no end in sight. This he did by examining himself, both his body and his mind, at the experiential level. As he went deeper and deeper into reflection and meditation, he saw that it was clinging to the five aggregates, i.e. the 'form' and the four components of the mind-consciousness, perception, sensation and reaction, which He called the 'five-aggregates of clinging, (*pañca-upādānakkhanda*), rooted in craving and born of ignorance that led to misery and suffering. Craving, clinging and attachment at the surface level, He observed, are augmented by greater misery at deeper levels.

People may be happy with what they have, but they always want something more. They develop attachment and become addicted to craving resulting in endless misery. It is like a bottomless pit, for, before long, one is attached to material things and identifies them as 'I, mine'. People do not stop there; they become attached also to beliefs, views, various theories and traditions and such among other things.

The Buddha out of compassion for the world exclaimed that the people of this world fall into trouble and sojourn on and on in *samsāra,* not knowing how to escape from their

misery. There must be an escape, which can be discerned.
The Buddha then looked at this age-old problem 'with careful
attention, resulting in a breakthrough with wisdom' He asked
himself as to why was there sorrow, lamentation, pain, grief,
ageing, decay and death. He saw that it was because of birth.
He next asked himself, 'Why birth? How does it come about?'
The reason for this too was very clear. It was due to becoming,
the urge to exist, to become, to come into being.

Let us look at these steps in the form of a chart, with
ageing, decay and death at the bottom, and then trace each
link upwards;

IGNORANCE
avijjā

VOLITIONAL FORMATIONS
saṅkkhāra

CONSCIOUSNESS
viññāṇa

MIND and MATTER
nāma-rūpa

SIX SENSES
salāyatana

SIX-FOLD CONTACT
phassa
FEELINGS-SENSATIONS

v*edanā*
CRAVING
taṇhā
CLINGING-GRASPING
upādāna

BECOMING/EXISTENCE
bhava

BIRTH
jāti

AGEING-DECAY-DEATH
jarā-maraṇa

'How did consciousness come about?' He realized that it was due to a specific condition, namely volitional activities. Mental volitional formations resulting from negative and positive intentions which is also equated to *kamma*. It is the sum-total of all of the unspent *kammic* energy which had been generated and accumulated in previous existences, the energies which had not been used up previously. 'Then why does one participate in volitional activities'? He asked himself, and He saw with insight and wisdom that it was due to ignorance (*avijjā*).

Beings act without realizing or knowing the consequences of their intentions and actions. In fact they do not know, nor understand the Four Noble Truths. They are also ignorant of the natural law of cause and effect, and ignorant of the consequences of negative *kamma*. Due to craving and clinging they are also ignorant of the ever-present dangers. It is the ignorance of the fact that there is no permanent entity called 'I' or self that is the root cause. This was as far as He needed to go.

The riddle of birth, life and death

Craving is conditioned by ignorance, while intense craving acts as a catalyst to ensure that one continues in the *saṁsāric* round of births and rebirths. Let us pause for a while and discuss feeling, craving and clinging a little more. **Feelings** are of three types: pleasant, unpleasant and neutral.

Craving. If there were no feelings or sensations, there would be no craving. This ideal situation is attained when one becomes a Noble One. But the rest of us are subject to greed, thirst, desire, longing, yearning and sensual wants. It is this craving that is the root cause of rebirth. Craving is of three types, namely:

> craving for sense-pleasures
> craving for rebecoming or existence
> craving for an end to existence.

"Where does craving arise and take root? Where there is the delightful and the pleasurable, there craving arises and takes root. Where there are forms, sounds, smells, tastes, bodily contacts and ideas, which are delightful and pleasurable, there craving arises and takes root." (D.22) Craving is conditioned not only by the pleasant, but by the unpleasant as well and those who suffer, be they the poor, the unloved, the sick, the aged, the disabled, the unwanted – all crave freedom from their suffering. Even the affluent and the healthy are not free from craving. They crave for more and more. Man's appetite for more and more is truly insatiable.

Clinging: Clinging or attachment is four-fold. There is attachment to sense-desires, to wrong or negative views, to rites and rituals as a saving grace and finally there is attachment to the self as an unchanging and continuing personality.

Clinging is not the mere attachment in a reasonable way to one's possessions and views, but the overly attachment and overly grasping and the consequent selfishness not to let go under any circumstance. Of the above the most dangerous and pernicious is the belief in an abiding self or an ego or 'I'. If this wrong notion is not got rid of, the discernment of the other two characteristics of existence, namely impermanence and suffering, becomes extremely difficult. On the other hand, if the wrong notion of a permanent 'self' is removed by proper application, the other wrong notions cease automatically. The Buddha saw no abiding indestructible soul or *atta*. He denied the existence of such an entity in the five aggregates: in this world of body and mind, or elsewhere.

"All this is void of an *atta* or derivatives thereof"
suññaṁ idaṁ attena va attaniyena vā (M.22).

"O Mogharaja, ever mindful – see the world as void
Having eradicated the notion of a self (*attā*) so may one overcome death:

sunnatā lokaṁ avekkhassu – Mogharāja sadā sato
attānudiṭṭhiṁ vohacca – evaṁ maccutaro siyā (Sn.1119).
We left the Buddha at the end of His conclusion that 'volitional

activities are conditioned by ignorance'. We can now continue from there: He then looked at what He had discovered in reverse order as well, and it confirmed His findings: "When there is no birth, ageing and death do not come to be. With the cessation of becoming, comes cessation of ageing and death. When there is no becoming, birth does not come to be. With cessation of existence, comes cessation of birth".... (And so on.).........up to ignorance. In other words, ageing and death resulted because of birth, which was because of becoming, the process of being born because of (and is conditioned by) clinging... .

These findings are what we know as dependent origination - *Paṭiccasamuppāda*. Let us read a few of the Buddha's own words on this subject as given in the *Nidāna Saṁyutta*.

i. *Origination*

"Bhikkhus, before my enlightenment, when I was yet a bodhisatta, not yet fully enlightened, it occurred to me: "Alas, this world has fallen into trouble, in that it is born, ages and dies, it passes away and is reborn, yet it does not understand the escape from this suffering (headed by) ageing-and-death?'

"Then it occurred to me: 'when what exists does ageing-and-death come to be? By what is ageing-and-death conditioned?' Then, bhikkhus, through careful attention, there took place in me a breakthrough by wisdom: 'When there is birth, ageing-and-death comes to be; ageing-and-death has birth as its condition.' "Then, bhikkhus, it occurred to me: 'when what exists does birth come to be? By what is birth conditioned? ... Then, bhikkhus, through careful attention, there took place in me a breakthrough by wisdom: 'When there is becoming, birth comes to be; birth has becoming as its condition..."

"Then, bhikkhus, it occurred to me: "Thus with ignorance as condition, volitional formations (come to be); with volitional formations as condition, consciousness..." Such is the origin of this whole mass of suffering. 'Origination, origination' – thus, bhikkhus, in regard to things unheard before there arose in me vision, knowledge, wisdom, true knowledge and light".

ii. *Cessation*

"Then, bhikkhus, it occurred to me: 'when what does not exist does ageing-and-death not come to be? With the cessation of what does the cessation of ageing-and-death come about?' Then, bhikkhus, through careful attention, there took place in me a breakthrough by wisdom: 'When there is no birth, ageing-and-death does not come to be; with the cessation of birth comes cessation of ageing-and-death.' "Then, bhikkhus, it occurred to me: "Thus with the remainderless fading away and cessation of ignorance comes cessation of volitional formations: with the cessation of volitional formations, cessation of consciousness ... Cessation, cessation – thus, bhikkhus, in regard to things unheard before there arose in me vision, knowledge, wisdom, true knowledge, and light." *Nidāna Saṁyutta.*

Dependent Origination (in direct order- *anuloma*)**

From **Ignorance** come volitional actions (leading to rebirth)
From **volitional** actions comes (rebirth) – consciousness
From (rebirth) **– consciousness** comes name and form (personality)
From **name and form** come the five senses and mind-base
From the **five senses** and mind-base comes contact
From **contact** come feelings (sensations)
From **feelings** (sensations) comes craving/desire
From **craving** comes clinging/grasping or attachment (to continued existence)
From **clinging/grasping** comes becoming
From **becoming** comes birth
From **birth** come ageing and death, sorrow, lamentation, pain, grief, and despair. Thus there is the origination of this whole mass of suffering.

Dependent Origination (in 'reverse' order: *paṭiloma*)

If **ignorance** is absent (there will be) no volitional activities
With no **volitional activities**, no rebirth-consciousness
With no **rebirth-consciousness** no name and form
With no **name and form**, no five senses and mind-base
With no **senses and mind-base**, no contact
With no **contact,** no feelings/sensations
With no **feelings/sensations**, no craving
With no **craving**, no clinging
With no **clinging,** no becoming
With no **becoming,** no birth

With no **birth,** ageing and death cease, and sorrow, lamentation, pain, grief and despair. Thus there is the cessation of this whole mass of suffering.

Another discovery of the Buddha was that consciousness finds nutriment in mind-and-matter, and mind-and-matter in turn finds nutriment in consciousness. They show a symbiotic relationship. This is reminiscent of the relationship between certain species of fungi and algae which can live together symbiotically by developing into lichens, which can then live even under harsh climatic conditions, but cannot survive independent of each other.

"... Therefore, Ānanda, this is the cause, source, origin, and condition for mentality-materiality, namely, consciousness. ..... Therefore, Ānanda, this is the cause, source, origin, and condition for consciousness, namely, materiality-mentality" ...(Mahā Nidāna Sutta). In the same Sutta the Buddha emphasized the importance of specificity as a linking factor in this chain of conditionality:

" ...Ānanda, if one is asked: 'Are ageing and death due to a specific condition?' one should say: 'They are'. If one is asked 'Through what condition is there ageing and death?' one should say: 'With birth as condition there is ageing and death'. Ānanda, if one is asked: 'Is birth due to a specific condition?' one should say: 'it is'. If one is asked: 'through what condition is there birth?' One should say: 'With becoming as condition there is birth'... "Thus, Ānanda, with mentality-materiality as condition there is consciousness; with consciousness as condition there is mentality-materiality; ... and with birth as a condition ageing and death, sorrow, lamentation, pain, grief, and despair come to be. Such is the origin of this entire mass of suffering."

When we looked at the diagrammatic representation of the twelve factors of dependent origination, we saw that each was conditioned by the preceding factor, which in turn conditioned the next and so on. Thus, for volitional formations the causal condition was ignorance. For consciousness it was volitional formations and so on. The Buddha explained it in this manner for the ease of memorisation and of comprehension. However, he has stated elsewhere that there are in fact twenty-four other conditions (*paccaya*) also contributing in various combinations to condition each of the twelve factors of dependent origination. It would suffice for our current discussion merely to note these relationships, feed back loops and dependence of its twelve factors by way of the twenty-four modes of conditionality[5].

We can now see that dependent origination is a teaching of conditionality, which encompasses everything in the cosmos, and that this teaching is the essence of the Buddha's Dhamma. Dependent origination and conditionality are facts of life.

If one were asked to summarise dependent origination, the obvious choice of words would be none other than those used by Arahat Assaji (one of the Buddha's first five disciples) when answering Upatissa's[6] query as to what was the Buddha's doctrine:

> *Ye dhammā hetupphabavā -*
> *tesaṁ hetuṁ tathāgato āha*
> *Tesaṁ ca yo nirodho -*
> *evaṁvādī mahāsamaṇo.*
> 'Whatever from a cause proceeds,

Thereof the Tathāgata has explained the cause:
Its cessation too He has explained:
This is the teaching of the Supreme Sage"

Vin.1.Mahāvagga

Conditionality goes on forever, uninterrupted and uncontrolled by any external agency or power of any sort.

Chapter IV

Understanding the Paṭiccasamuppāda

In the previous chapter was presented the doctrine of dependent origination the way the Buddha discovered it and in the manner in which he explained it. This was based on a number of discourses of the Buddha. We left aside the more complex details, for our purpose was simply to get the feel of this important subject.

The Buddha emphatically declared that the first beginning of existence is inconceivable. It is impossible to think or believe in a first beginning because no one can truly trace the ultimate origin of anything, not even of a grain of sand, let alone of human beings, – despite what present-day cosmologists are wont to say.

It should be realized that life is just a 'becoming'. It is merely a conflux of mind and body subject to conditionality. According to the Buddha, all conditioned or compounded things come into being, presently exist and then cease – *uppāda, ṭhiti and bhaṅga.*

However, for us to fully understand this profound subject, we need to review the information and explanations given in chapter 2, plus the additional information given below. Even then, no explanation can be expected to give a full and final understanding of the process of dependent origination.

Nevertheless, the information contained here can be used to probe the process while at the same time train the mind to come to a reasonable understanding of this profound and fundamental doctrine.

One of the links of the *paṭiccasamuppāda* which frequently bothers people is the difficulty in visualizing how "volitional formations/*kamma* in one life conditions consciousness" in the next. Consciousness is the most subtle and deep point which is difficult to grasp and comprehend, for it is this link that explains rebecoming and rebirth. And this is what He told Ānanda: "If consciousness were not to descend into the mother's womb, would mentality-materiality take shape in the womb?" "Certainly not venerable Sir."

"If, after descending into the womb, consciousness were to expire, would mentality-materiality be generated into this present state of being?" "Certainly not, venerable Sir."...

"Therefore, Ananda, this is the cause, the source, the origin, and condition for mentality-materiality, namely, conscious-ness:" *Mahā Nidāna Sutta.*

The rebirth-consciousness, which we are discussing here is explained in the Abhidhamma as follows: For rebirth consciousness to take place, it must be preceded by death in the immediate previous existence. Death-consciousness or *cuti-citta* is the very last consciousness to occur at the moment of death. It is the *citta* which marks the exit from a particular life. Death-consciousness is of the same type as the rebirth-linking consciousness and moment-to-moment consciousness (*bhavaṅga*), and like them it pertains to the process-freed side of existence, the passive flow of consciousness outside an active cognitive process. Death-consciousnss is followed by a rebirth-linking consciousness called the *paṭisandhi-citta* which occurs only once in any individual existence. It is at the moment of rebirth and is conditioned immediately by the previous death-consciousness.

This rebirth-linking consciousness is followed by the usual moment-to-moment consciousness (*bhavaṅga*), which continues to be present throughout a person's life. It is different from the consciousness which arises when the six-sense bases in a live person come into contact with their respective sense-objects as follows:

"With eye and forms arises visual consciousness
With ear and sounds arises auditory consciousness
With nose and odours arises olfactory consciousness
With tongue and flavours arises taste consciousness
With body and tangibles arises tactile consciousness
With mind and mental objects arises mind-conscious-
ness" (M,I,111-112).

At that time, when perception, sensation and reaction are operative, the *bhavaṅga* consciousness lies dormant and comes into effect immediately thereafter. (Please also see chapter 2). In the proposition, volitional formations/*kamma* conditions consciousness, we have to understand that *saṅkhāra* is equated to *kamma* and that the consciousness referred to here is rebirth-consciousness.

To understand this subject better, it is necessary first to have an understanding of energy systems. We are aware that every phenomenon in the cosmos is based on energy and accordingly we generate energy whenever we think or do anything. This energy is what we can equate to *kamma* and this accumulated *kammic* energy gets attenuated to different degrees when a person attains the three transcendental paths of stream-winner, once-returner and non-returner respectively. It comes to an end with the attainment of the fourth transcendental path, which is Arahatship.

However, for the life processes to continue too, energy is necessary. And we know that mitochondria, which generate energy for vital activities are in all the cells of our body. And such energy falls within the domain of physical energy.

In the case of human conception too, like in all human activities, energy is necessary, which fact embryologists know when they carry out *in-vitro* fertilization. Perhaps the same type of system prevails in the human body too when *in-vivo* fertilization takes place. In other words, energy is required at the point of conception. The question then is, 'where does this energy come from'? Is it from within the uterus, or could it be from the energy of rebirth-consciousness and *kamma*?

So let us picture what may perhaps happen when a person is about to die. According to dependent origination, it is the accumulated *kamma* of the previous birth that acts as the specific condition for rebirth-linking consciousness in the next. The consciousness, which we are now discussing is the rebirth-linking consciousness which is the first consciousness that appears in the new life, i.e. in the zygote at the moment of its initiation.

According to the Dhamma, three conditions must be present for a new life to come into being. They are the viable spermatozoon of the father, a viable ovum (oocyte) of the mother and the 'person-to-be-born'. The energy to trigger the start of a new life is presumably provided by the person-to-be-born, called *gandhabba* in the *Mahātaṇhāsaṁkhaya Sutta*.

Some *sutta*-commentators believe that 'gandhabba'[1] is simply a term for rebirth-consciousness or *paṭisandhi viññāṇa*. It is this energy potential released at the time a person dies in the previous birth and conditioned by craving is the desire for becoming. This energy is so formidable that it attracts itself to another appropriate existence. It is the last thought-process that carries with it this grasping force (energy) and the unused *kamma* and, like a flash of lightning, it enters the mother's womb, and perhaps enters the oocyte simultaneously with the spermatozoon and energizes the male and female pro-nuclei in the zygote to undergo the first mitotic cell division, thus laying the foundation for the start of a new life. The two-celled embryo then divides itself into a four, eight, and sixteen-cell embryo and so on.

Unless rebirth-consciousness links up with the zygote at its initiation, there can be no start of a new life. Along with this consciousness the rest of the factors of mentality, as well as the physical factors of materiality, begin to manifest.

"This reciprocal conditional relationship between consciousness and name-and-form (*nāma-rūpa*) continues throughout the entire course of life; consciousness infuses the whole mental and material structure to make them participants in all experience; and the mental and material structure provide a footing for consciousness to grow and flourish." Bhikkhu Bodhi.

In ancient commentaries this transfer of consciousness and *kamma* is compared to what happens when one lighted candle is used to light another candle. Nothing substantial moves from one candle to the other, but the light does.

In understanding the above example we should keep in mind that nothing of the five aggregates (which we call a 'being'), moves from the previous life to the present one. Only conditionality exists. The Buddha has emphasized this as shown in the following incident:

Sāti was a recalcitrant monk who had insisted on misconstruing the Buddha's words. Sāti had insisted that consciousness is a persistent transmigrating entity. The Buddha had then reaffirmed His previous statement that consciousness is dependently arisen in that it arises in dependence of conditions and that apart from conditions there can be no origination of consciousness *(aññātra paccayā natthi viññaṇassa sambhavo)*.

Getting back to human development, it is seen that once the embryo is initiated, it will start developing rapidly and by the third week will show the initiation of the heart and circulation system as well as the start of the formation of the brain and the nervous system. This is followed rapidly by the formation of the five physical sense-organs and consciousness, namely the eyes, ears, nose, tongue, body and the mental-base *(ajjhattika)*, and their respective external *(bāhira)* bases which are: visible objects, sound, odour, taste, body and mind objects. The ensuing mind-body phenomenon reaches foetal maturity at the end of nine months.

The arising of the above primordial mind-body combination during embryonic and foetal development, as well as the continuing development during the course of life, is called the 'round of results' *(vipākavaṭṭa)*, and is the result of our past volitions-*kamma*. The microscopic zygote thus finally develops into a human being equipped with a six-sense base, during the foetal-embryonic stage. It is perhaps useful to remember that when we referred to rebirth-linking consciousness, we did not imply that this consciousness is a

permanent entity, which continues in the same state without
change throughout the cycle of existence. Consciousness too
is conditioned and is therefore not permanent. It comes into
being, performs and passes away yielding place to a new
consciousness. It is explained as a perpetual stream that goes
on until the final cessation of 'becoming'. When one gives it
more thought, one realizes that in effect there is no 'being'
in this world in the absence of consciousness, and in a way,
consciousness is existence, the will to live, to continue and
to become (*bhava*).

We can now see that the *paṭiccasamuppāda* is a teaching
of conditionality of everything in the world. It goes on forever,
uninterrupted and uncontrolled by any external agency or
power of any sort.

Let us make a chart once again of the twelve links forming
the chain, the spiral of continuing existence.   The following
list (reading downwards) denotes the conditional relationship
between the 12 links of dependently arising phenomena.

Ignorance	
Volitional Formations	past life
Consciousness	
Mentality-Materiality	
Six Senses	
Contact	Present life
Feeling	
Craving	
Clinging	
Becoming	

Birth
Ageing and Death   next life

In the doctrine of dependent origination, we refer to three periods of time: the past, the present and the future. This is in order to exemplify how the twelve factors act upon the consecutive sequence of lives. Ignorance and volitional formations belong to the previous birth, the next eight links to the present, and the last two links, birth and ageing and death belong to the next existence. Now, how can this chain of cause and effect be broken in order to reach liberation? Unless we can break the chain, we will surely drift forever in *saṁsāra*, in a stream of birth, death and rebirth.

The Buddha in His wisdom explored all the possibilities and realized that there were, in fact, two points along this chain where it could be broken. Of these, the first is 'ignorance' and the other is at the point of 'craving.' He therefore, had to find a way to stop craving. He recollected that by meditating with insight, wisdom and equanimity, one could develop total awareness of every sensation which occurs in the body. When one sees every sensation without greed, hatred or delusion, one does not react to situations.

The Buddha has also shown us a way out of ignorance, which in turn will prevent the arising of fresh reactions. This is by means of *vipassanā* meditation, for, with continued *vipassanā* meditation it is possible for us to develop mindfulness and insight. Then will arise wisdom with which we can successfully eradicate ignorance. Liberation follows.

This is how an enlightened being, an Arahant, faces all incidents in his day-to-day life: with wisdom and without volition. Having eliminated conceiving the Arahant no longer finds delight in the objects he encounters. He no longer pursues pleasure and enjoyment and in the absence of delight and craving, there is no condition for the renewal of *saṁsāric* existence. At the end of his present life, he concludes his journey in *saṁsāra* and brings an end to it.

We have so far depicted dependent origination as a chain of causes and effects strung over time. However, this is not necessarily the best way to show causal inter-connectedness.

The Buddha has said:
> When this is, that is.
> From the arising of this, that arises.
> When this is not, that is not.
> From the ceasing of this, that ceases.

Mahātaṇhāsaṅkhaya sutta.

A recent commentator sees in the above: "an inter-play of synchronic and linear principles". The linear principle connects events over time as follows:

> When this is, that is
> When this is not, that is not.

On the other hand, the synchronic principle is also evident as follows:

> From the arising of this, that arises
> From the ceasing of this, that ceases.

It is then evident that the two principles intersect so that any given event is influenced by two sets of conditions, those acting from the past, and those acting from the present"[2].

Dependent Origination and the Four Noble Truths

There are many ways to show the interconnectedness between the twelve links of the Dependent Origination and the four Noble Truths. For instance, in one analysis it is shown that the first Noble Truth, (the existence of suffering or unsatisfactoriness), is related to the links of consciousness, name and form, the six-sense bases, contact, sensation, birth, ageing and death. The balance five links of ignorance, reaction, craving, clinging and becoming are related to the second Noble Truth (the origin of suffering).

We can then say that the latter set of five are the causal factors, while the former set of seven are the effective factors. We thus see that it is the origin of suffering which causes suffering, for suffering is dependent on its origin and will not exist in its absence.

It is also possible to show that, in the doctrine of dependent origination, all four Noble Truths are embodied: "The *paṭiccasamuppāda* in its order of arising manifests the process of becoming (*bhava*): in other words, the appearance of suffering (the First Truth); and how this process of becoming or suffering is conditioned (the Second Truth). In its order of ceasing, the *paṭiccasamuppāda* makes plain the cessation of this becoming, this suffering (the Third Truth), and how it ceases (the Fourth Truth)"[3].

Chapter V

Paṭiccasamuppāda and the *Upanisā Sutta*

To study and comprehend the *paṭiccasamuppāda*, it is important that there be a total immersion in this *sutta*. It requires a "paradigm shift". We need to look at it not merely as a doctrine but as something personal, which one can experience. By doing so, it comes alive. We also need this focus not only in regard to this doctrine, but also to all doctrines of the Buddha, for He spoke only of 'suffering and how to end suffering.' In fact, when we look at the twelve links, we see that the last few words in the *sutta* refer to 'this whole mass of suffering'.

Hence, the purpose of understanding this *sutta* is to find a solution, a way to end this otherwise ceaseless wandering in *saṁsāra*. If we lose track of this fundamental point, we would only be looking at the byways and not at the main highway to Nibbāna.

Let us examine what we have learnt and understood by looking at the twelve links in the standard descending order, as if we are the live participants in this *saṁsāric* process of the rounds of rebirths. In the discussion which follows, 'I' and 'we' are used in the conventional sense merely as expedients (much like the way the Buddha referred to his previous births).

Starting with ignorance, we looked at how we had perhaps conducted ourselves in our previous birth, which, for purposes of discussion, we assumed was here on earth. We believed that conditioned by our ignorance of the dangers inherent in the three fundamental evils of greed, aversion and delusion, and not understanding the three eternal verities of impermanence, suffering and the absence of a permanent 'I' or 'self', we remained unaware that there was no permanent self or 'I'. We also had no knowledge of the working of the immanent law of *kamma* and rebirth. In fact, we did not know the four Noble Truths. As a result, we accumulated a considerable amount of negative *kamma*.

On the other hand, although we were not aware of the above factors of defilements, we were inherently good people, for we had perhaps been kind, compassionate, sharing, forbearing, patient and also morally above reproach in our previous birth. Consequently, we did spiritually evolve a little more and became 'eligible' for an earth life because the accumulated positive *kamma* outweighed the negative *kamma*. Therefore, when we died, we received another chance to spiritually evolve further by birth in this world of sentient beings. We are now reaping some of the 'benefits' of our *kamma*, as *kamma-vipāka* or in other words the consequences of our previous actions in *saṁsāra*.

This earthly life did not come about fortuitously, but conditioned by our previous volitions *(kamma)*. We now have a chance to progress in our evolution and hopefully can move closer to liberation if we get rid of ignorance, greed, hatred and delusion, and practise generosity, morality and the four sublime states of loving-kindness, compassion, participating joy and equanimity. We now also have the opportunity to understand dependent origination as a way out of ignorance.

It has become clear to us how rebirth-consciousness appears at the time of conception in the mother's womb in this re-becoming and we then pictured how mind-and-matter develops in the embryo and the foetus, followed by the development of the six-sense organs and the related six-sense-consciousnesses. We then came to appreciate that although we had considered ourselves as unique entities we are, in fact, nothing but body and mind, which together comprise the five aggregates of clinging. There is no permanent 'I'.

We saw how, because of the six-fold contact of our senses with their respective objects, we started to have feelings, which turned to craving and then clinging and how we could become enslaved to our cravings and clingings. We also saw how the energy so generated would lead to our wanting survival or becoming or existence: in other words, giving way to the atavistic tendency for survival and perpetuation of the species.

If during this lifetime we are to find a way out of the *saṁsāric* round, we need to mend our ways. We need to not only get rid of our inherent tendency towards craving, but to eradicate it totally.

> 'Just as a tree with roots untouched and firm in the
>   ground
> Though felled, puts forth new shoots,
> If the habit of craving and aversion is not uprooted,
> Suffering arises over and over again' (Dh.338).

If we do not get rid of attachment, craving, clinging and hatred along with our delusion of a permanent self, we will at the end of this existence be merely drifting once more in *saṁsāra* and be subject to the whole mass of suffering. We, therefore, have understood that we need to step back and mindfully change direction, change course and adopt one of the proven methods of the Buddha to develop wisdom and thereby attain liberation.

However, to develop wisdom, it is necessary to understand the Dhamma, and this we can do by reading or listening to the Dhamma and practising it, which would result in *sutamaya-paññā*. (In the present context it is repeatedly reading and understanding this book). Then by reflection and contemplation, we can gain the wisdom called *cintāmaya-paññā*. This will finally lead us to insight or *vipassanā* meditation and, through insight meditation, we should be able to achieve wisdom – *bhāvanāmayā-paññā* and comprehension of the Dhamma (Ch1).

How can we, after studying and understanding the *paṭiccasamuppāda*, take the next step? How can we get rid of ignorance, craving and clinging and achieve liberation? Fortunately, the Buddha has indeed shown us how this can be done stepwise. He has shown us how we can move from mundane dependent origination to the supra-mundane state by a series of interconnected links leading to liberation (*vimutti*).

Upanisā sutta

This advice is found in the *Upanisā sutta* of the *Saṁyutta Nikāya*. In this *sutta*, the Buddha begins with the words, "The destruction of taints, monks, is for one who knows and sees, not for one who does not know and does not see..."

Taints are what are commonly called *āsavas* in the *suttas*, and there are four groups of them:

> sense-desires, - *kāma-āsava*
> desire for existence - *bhava-āsava*
> holding narrow views - *diṭṭhi-āsava*,
> ignorance- *avijjā-āsava*.

What are the benefits of removing these taints? It is the realization of Nibbāna.

It is said that with stream-entry - *sotāpanna*, the taint of wrong-views is destroyed. Through the path of Non-returning - *anāgāmi,* the taint of sense-desire is destroyed, and through the path of *Arahantship* the rest of the taints of existence and ignorance are finally destroyed.

The relevant portion of the *Upanisā sutta* reads as follows:

... "Thus, bhikkhus, with ignorance as the proximate cause, volitional formations (come to be); with volitional formations as proximate cause, consciousness; with consciousness as proximate cause, name-and-form; with name-and-form as proximate cause, the six sense bases; with the six sense bases as proximate cause, contact; with contact as proximate cause, feeling; with feeling as proximate cause, craving; with craving as proximate cause, clinging; with clinging as proximate cause, birth; with birth as proximate cause, suffering; with suffering as proximate cause, confidence; with confidence as proximate cause, gladness; with gladness as proximate cause, rapture: with rapture as proximate cause, tranquillity; with tranquillity as proximate cause, happiness; with happiness as proximate cause, concentration; with concentration as proximate cause,

knowledge and vision of things as they really are; with
knowledge and vision of things as they really are as proximate
cause, revulsion; with revulsion as proximate cause, dispassion;
with dispassion as proximate cause, liberation; with liberation
as proximate cause, the knowledge of destruction (of the
āsavas)".

It is seen from the above that the way to liberation begins
with confidence initially supported by *ignorance* and ends
with *āsavakkhaya-ñāṇa*, meaning the wisdom for the
destruction of taints by attaining *vimutti*, liberation or
Arahantship.

To study transcendental dependent origination, we can
depict the links in the *Upanisā sutta* in the same manner in
which we displayed the twelve links of the *paṭiccasamuppāda*
in chapter 3:

The *Upanisā Sutta*

Part1.Mundane dependent origination

Ignorance *(avijjā)* leads to .... *kamma* formations *(saṅkhāra)*
Kamma leads to .... consciousness *(viññāṇa)*
Consciousness leads to. .... mentality-materiality *(nāma-rūpa)*
Mentality-materality leads to ... six-fold sense bases
    (salāyatana)
Six-fold sense bases lead to.... ....contact *(phassa)*
Contact leads to.................. feeling *(vedanā)*
Feeling leads to................... craving *(taṇhā)*
Craving leads to................. clinging *(upādāna)*

Clinging leads to.................. .. existence (*bhava*)
Existence leads to................ .. .. birth (*jāti*)
Birth leads to .... suffering (*dukkha*)

Part 2. Supra-mundane dependent origination

Suffering leads to .... confidence (*saddhā*)
Confidence leads to .... joy/gladness (*pāmojja*)
Gladness/Joy leads to .... rapture (*pīti*)
Rapture leads to...................tranquillity (*passaddhi*)
Tranquillity leads to ....happiness (*sukha*)
Happiness leads to .... concentration (*samādhi*)
Concentration leads to.................knowledge and vision of
      things as they really are (*yathābhūta-ñāṇadassana*)
Knowledge and vision leads to .....revulsion/disenchantment
      (*nibbidā*)
Revulsion-disenchantment leads to ..dispassion (*virāga*)
Dispassion leads to .... liberation (*vimutti*)
Liberation leads to ....destruction of cankers or
      taints (*āsavakkaya- ñāṇa*)

When we look at the *Upanisā sutta* in the above form, we
see in part one, the now familiar twelve links of dependent
origination, which we had studied before in chapter 3. The
only difference is in the 12th link, where the Buddha has
purposefully replaced "death and decay" with "suffering". For
it is this substitution, which helps to lead to the second
application (part 2) of dependent arising, which is to show a
path leading to liberation.

Part two begins with, confidence *(saddhā)*, i.e., confidence in the Buddha and his doctrines, and then leads up to tranquillity and happiness. From there on are shown the progressive steps leading finally to liberation and with it the destruction of taints. This second application of 'dependent arising' has been given the name 'transcendental or supramundane dependent arising' as it leads to transcendence[1].

It appears that in the second part of this *sutta*, the Buddha is telling us not to stop but to move forward till we are fully liberated (*vimutti*) and all cankers/taints (*āsava*) are destroyed. For, by now, having comprehended the doctrine of dependent origination, and understood conditionality experientially, the learner is suffused with confidence and acceptance of the Truth in the Buddha Dhamma. He should now wish to go forward. This decision in turn will generate joy or gladness in the meditator, who also knows that he is proceeding in the right direction.

At this stage, the meditator would check within him as to whether his morality is completely above reproach and whether he is practising the *sīla* portion of the Noble Eightfold Path. When this is self-confirmed, the meditator will be suffused with rapture and will make a determined effort to proceed intensively through the concentration and wisdom groups of the Noble Eightfold Path.

He would now realize that further progress is not possible without *vipassanā* meditation. The links of joy, rapture, tranquillity, happiness, concentration, knowledge-and-vision-of-things as-they-are, disenchantment and dispassion- (*pāmojja, pīti, passadhi, sukha, samādhi, yathābhūta-ñāṇa-dassana, nibbidā and dispassion* respectively (as shown in the *Upanisā sutta*), are states of mind. They are sequential steps in spiritual development leading to transcendence. They also act as signposts, which help identify our progress along the path to liberation *(vimutti)*.

We should also understand that each of the above steps arises in dependence on the previous one, and hence represents dependent origination, and demonstrates in the *Upanisā sutta* how they lead to dispassion and liberation.

There are also a number of *suttas* scattered in the *Sutta Piṭaka*[2], which show steps similar to those shown in the *Upanisā sutta* leading to liberation, but with individual variations, for, there are many ways to reach the goal. Some of the pathways are long and some are short. But the main signposts along the way remain the same, for we already know (chapter 3) that the Buddha varied his methods of teaching according to circumstances. The *Upanisā sutta* was directly addressed to his bhikkhus, who we can assume were already familiar with *vipassanā* meditation. All he needed therefore to do was merely to highlight the most important steps leading to liberation and leave it to the bhikkhus to fill in the gaps.

Vipassanā meditation

We are now living in a different era separated from the time of the Buddha by well over two thousand five hundred years. Hence it is difficult to find genuine *vipassanā* meditation masters. Two renowned 20th century masters were the late Mahasi Sayadaw[3] and the late Ñāṇārāma Mahāthera[4]. They had researched a vast amount of Buddhist literature including the *suttas,* commentaries and sub-commentaries on them as well as the monumental classical works, *Vissuddhi magga*[5] and the *Paṭisambhidā magga*[6] and incorporated such information into their own experiences in insight meditation practices before offering practical courses in *vipassanā* meditation.

The progressive steps in *vipassanā* meditation as taught and practised by them are given below in the form of a table. The steps are longer than those shown in the *Upanisā Sutta*. This is understandable; the present generation readers and meditators could very well benefit from more detailed instructions than their counterparts of twenty-five centuries ago, who had direct access to the Buddha or His Arahants.

Comparing steps to liberation through insight (*vipassanā*) meditation

(i) Mahasi Sayadaw

1. Analytical knowledge of mind and body
2. Knowledge by discerning conditionality
3. Knowledge of comprehension
4. Knowledge of corruption of insight
5. Knowledge of dissolution
6. Awareness of fearfulness
7. Knowledge of misery
8. Knowledge of disenchantment
9. Knowledge of desire for deliverance
10. Knowledge of re-observation
11. Knowledge of equanimity about formations
12. Insight leading to emergence

13.   Knowledge of adaptation
14.   Maturity knowledge
15.   Path knowledge
16.   Fruition knowledge
17.   Reviewing knowledge
18.   Attainment of fruition

(From: *The progress of insight* —
Mahasi Sayadaw)

(ii) Ñāṇārāma Mahathera

1.   Stage of viewing

i.   Discerning delimitation of mind and matter
ii.   Discernment of conditions
iii. Purification by overcoming doubt
iv.   Full understanding of the known

2. Stage of comprehension

i.   Knowledge of comprehension of the three
characteristics (impermanence-distress-no 'I')
ii.   Immature stage of knowledge of rise and fall of
phenomena
iii. Knowledge of corruptions of insight
iv.   Knowledge of right and wrong paths
v.   Mature knowledge of rise and fall of phenomena
vi.   Awareness of fearfulness
vii. Purification by knowledge and vision of the way

3. Stage of gaining insight

i. Knowledge of dissolution
ii. Knowledge of fearfulness
iii. Knowledge of danger
iv. Knowledge of disenchantment/revulsion
v. Knowledge of desire for deliverance
vi. Knowledge of reflection i.e., reviewing the three characteristics.
vii. Knowledge of equanimity towards formations
viii. Knowledge of conformity of all phenomena to the three characteristics
ix. Knowledge of change of lineage from mundane to supramundane (lineage of the noble ones)
x. Knowledge of path of stream-entry
xi. Knowledge of fruition

(From: *The Seven Contemplations of Insight* — Ñāṇārāma Mahāthera)

Voyage of Discovery

It is now time to re-state what we have discovered on our voyage through our body and mind, and what more needs to be done to achieve liberation.

Primary

a. Understood how mind and matter worked.
b. Learnt to cultivate mindfulness.
c. Changed lifestyle so as to ensure adherence to the *sīla* group of the Noble Eightfold Path and became

appreciative of the benefits of non-greed, non-hatred and non-delusion.

d. Commenced cultivating the sublime states of universal-kindness, compassion, unenvious-joy and equanimity *(mettā, karuṇā, muditā and upekkhā)*.

e. Studied the *paṭiccasamuppāda* and understood its interconnectedness to the Four Noble Truths and the doctrine of *kamma* and rebirth.

f. Made the *paṭiccasamuppāda* come alive during contemplation and discovered within it impermanence, unsatisfactoriness and the non-self nature of all phenomena at the transcendental level.

g. Practised reflection and contemplation.

Secondary

a. Developed a desire to go forward, and therefore discovered the *Upanisā Sutta* which shows the road to transcendence.

b. Understood and comprehended the *Upanisā Sutta* at the *sutamaya* and *cintāmaya* levels.

c. Realized that the links in the second part of the *Upanisā Sutta* directed us towards liberation and that insight *(vipassanā)* meditation is essential for further progress.

Tertiary

a. Realized that we have still some way to go on our journey to fruition.

b. Realized that *vipassanā* meditation required intensive application.

c. Looked around for a recognized teacher and/or books on *vipassanā* meditation, and commenced *vipassanā* meditation proper.

d. Observed that after reaching the 'concentration' stage, it was necessary to open one's mind to all phenomena as they appear and disappear.

e. Saw superficially the appearance and disappearance of phnomena.

* * * * * *

Some practical instructions on *vipassanā* meditation and how our knowledge and insight into the *paṭiccasamuppāda* could help us to complete our journey to liberation are offered in the next chapter.

Chapter VI

Paṭiccasamuppāda and *Vipassanā*
Meditation

We are now ready for the final part of our journey, for we now know and understand that everything in the universe is conditioned and subject to impermanence, distress and unsatisfactoriness and that there is no such thing as a continuing self or 'I'.

Life is a continuing process of evolution. Each of us has the potential to evolve morally and spiritually. In fact, we have been doing so during our journey through *saṁsāra* every time we have had an earthly life. We now have the added advantage of a time period in which the Buddha's Dhamma is available to guide us. This opportunity is not accidental but a result of the *pāramis*[1] which we had developed to a certain level in previous births.

If this were not true, we would not even have had the inclination or the opportunity to select this book for reading, let alone studying and comprehending its contents.

We now have complete confidence in the Buddha and the Dhamma, and are eager to experience the truth embodied in the *paṭiccasamuppāda,* for we have realized that craving, clinging and attachment are the byproducts of ignorance, which ensure our continuing journey in *saṁsāra.*

A special effort is needed to truly comprehend and realize the supramundane in a short series of steps. These steps are incorporated into the practice of *vipassanā* meditation, but to take these steps we have to promise ourselves that we shall make a sustained effort, for we are now well aware of the rewards that lie ahead. We can therefore perhaps repeat what the poet Robert Frost (1874-1963) said:

> "But I have promises to keep,
> ... And miles to go before I sleep"
> From: "Stopping by Woods on a Snowy Evening".

The time has come for this effort. However, this last part of the journey has to be crafted carefully and followed conscientiously.

The Buddha has repeatedly emphasized the importance of contemplation and meditation as a way, in fact an essential requirement, to achieve liberation. The classical *suttas* in this regard are *The Mahā Satipaṭṭhāna sutta* (M) we referred to in chapter 2, the *Ānāpānasati sutta* (M) and the *Upanisā sutta* with which we became familiar in the previous chapter.

There are now numerous meditation centers in the USA, UK, Europe and Asia that conduct courses on a regular basis in the Theravada tradition and are popularly known as *vipassanā* meditation centers. The focus is on strictly following the instructions as contained in the *Satipaṭṭhāna Sutta*. The courses range from 1-3 months of total immersion, or shorter retreats of ten days' total immersion, as well as still shorter workshops. The teachers at these centers are second or third generation descendents of the original *vipassanā* meditation masters who are said to have individually 're-discovered' *vipassanā* meditation techniques in Myanmar *(Burma)* and used them with success to attain liberation.

The need for the earnest student to find a suitable meditation teacher must be emphasized. Even if the reader is very knowledgeable in the Buddha Dhamma, the fact remains that one is now journeying along an unfamiliar path. Consequently, there will be many occasions when one could benefit from the advice and instructions of a competent, experienced meditation master.

It is also advisable for the student to enquire whether such a teacher uses an understanding and contemplation of the *paṭiccasamuppāda* with its twelve links as an essential part of the *vipassanā* practice, for we can recollect from our previous studies what the Buddha has said in this regard:

"He who sees dependent origination sees the Dhamma, He who sees the Dhamma sees the dependent origination" (M28).

Then by inference, could we not perhaps say 'one who does not see dependent origination does not see the Dhamma' and 'he who does not see the Dhamma does not see dependent origination'?

But while the reader is searching for a teacher, he may perhaps find the information given below sufficient to start meditating in the *vipassanā* way. **It should however be kept in mind that these instructions are poor substitutes for a competent and proven meditation guide.** The instructions given below are drawn from the limited experiences of my fellow meditators and myself.

Preliminary steps in meditation

The beginner must first feel sufficiently motivated to proceed on his own. He should dedicate himself earnestly to the task ahead. Next he has to select a place suitable for his daily meditation and decide on a time frame for each meditation session. (He can of course change this as he moves along and as his competency improves). Further, he has to select a suitable place relatively free of disturbances. Then, by experimentation, he must choose a suitable posture in which he can remain for a considerable length of time with the minimum of bodily movements. He also needs to have the patience to continue in the practice even when there are no visible signs of progress. In summary, the meditator needs to find each day, the time followed by the following 6 p's:

Time - place - posture - practice - patience - perseverance - and still more practice!

A person may find it beneficial to start a meditation session by first looking inwards and ensuring that he is skilful in speech, action and livelihood (steps in the Noble Eightfold Path).

The usual practice is then to arrive at a sublime and a tranquil state of mind by wishing himself and all sentient beings to be happy and well. By doing so, he is able, at least for the duration of the meditation session, to suppress the negativities of anger and greed. The tool to be used is often called an 'invocation' or a 'wish'. The meditator himself can formulate it, or the following model (or a modification) could be used instead. Most *vipassanā* teachers suggest this kind of invocation to be used by their students.

A Wish For Happiness

May I be well. May I be happy and peaceful. May no harm come to me.

May I be free from greed, selfishness and jealousy. May I be able to meet the ups and down of life with patience, courage and understanding.

May my parents, teachers and family be well. May they be happy and peaceful. May no harm come to them. May they be free from greed, selfishness and jealousy. May they be able to meet the ups and downs of life with patience, courage and understanding.

May my friends and all the people in this city be well. May they be happy and peaceful. May no harm come to them. May they be free from greed, selfishness and jealousy. May they be able to meet the ups and downs of life with patience, courage and understanding.

May everyone in this country be well. May they be happy and peaceful. May no harm come to them. May they be free from greed, selfishness and jealousy. May they be able to meet the ups and downs of life with patience, courage and understanding.

May those who dislike me be well. May they be happy and peaceful. May no harm come to them. May they be free from greed, selfishness and jealousy. May they be able to face the ups and downs of life with patience, courage and understanding.

May all sentient beings be well. May they be happy and peaceful. May no harm come to them. May they be free from greed, selfishness and jealousy. May they be able to

**meet the ups and downs of life with patience, courage
and understanding.**

He now tells himself to exercise self-restraint in respect of
his six-sense faculties: eyes, ears, tongue, nose, body and
mind, and after gathering inward confidence to commence
meditation. If he were now to focus his mind on one or more
of the 'sublime states' (*brahma-vihāra*) of universal kindness
(*mettā*), compassion *(karuṇā)*, participating joy (*muditā*) and
equanimity (*upekkhā*), he would find that his mind would
settle down and reach a high degree of tranquillity and serenity
conducive to meditation, because:

Universal kindness or friendliness promotes good-will and
therefore reduces ill-will.

Compassion results in reducing the pain and misery of others
in a practical way. It helps abandon cruelty, while encouraging
us to be merciful and helpful.

Participating joy fosters absence of envy and helps abandon
hatred and dislike.

Equanimity helps us to regard all persons with tolerance and
it generates goodness in us.

These four emotions, as we can see, are the embodiment of
goodness. That is why they are called 'sublime'.

William Shakespeare (1564-1616) was not far off the mark
when he said:

"The quality of mercy is not strained
It droppeth as the gentle rain from heaven
Upon the place beneath: it is twice blessed
It blesseth him that gives and him that takes".

We only need replace the word 'mercy' with friendliness, compassion, sympathetic joy or equanimity respectively.

And, when we reflect even for a moment on the ups and downs of life, we will undoubtedly agree with the nineteenth century anonymous poet who wrote:

"Life is mostly froth and bubbles,
Two things stand like stone:
Kindness in another's troubles
Courage in your own."

From. 1866 - 'Ye wearie wayfarer
Hys Ballad. In Eight Fyttes'

Now with a non-agitated mind, the meditator can take the next step, which is to develop concentration.

Concentration

Since the meditator is firmly established in morality (*sīla*), and has a tranquil mind, he can now select a subject on which to fix his attention to the exclusion of other thoughts during a meditation session. One of the most popular subjects used for developing concentration is one's breath, for when it comes to the breath, one does not associate it with anything, not even with oneself or 'I'. One considers the breath as something that has always been there from the day of birth to the last breath on the day of his death.

In the meditation on the breath, the posture is particularly important. If one does not adopt an upright cross-legged, or semi-cross-legged posture sleepiness can often hinder one's efforts. (Western meditators may find that they are unable to adopt this posture for physiological or other reasons, in which case, sitting upright on a straight-backed chair with the feet firmly placed on the ground has been found by present day meditation teachers to give comparable results). The meditator now focuses his attention on his normal breath and watches how the air flows in and out through his nostrils. He follows the breath only at the point of entry and exit. Following points will be useful:

> i. The first step is to find it. What we are looking for is the physical sensation of the air that passes in and out of the nostrils. This is usually just inside the tip of the nose, and less frequently on the upper lip. You find your 'point' by taking a deep breath and noticing where you have the most distinct sensation of the in-breath. Repeat with an out-breath and confirm this point. It is from this point that you will follow the whole breath.

Once you have located this 'breath point,' don't deviate from it.

> ii. Make no attempt to control the breath.

> iii. Observe the breath closely. There are delicate variations. Long breaths, short breaths, deep breaths,

shallow breaths, smooth breaths and ragged breaths. They also combine in various ways - like the notes in a piece of music.

iv. Next, do not observe only the outline of the breath. Observe the beginning, middle and the end.   So also in the out-breath.

v. Study the above phenomena and move on. Return your attention to the breath, over and over again.

vi. Do not let the monkey-mind syndrome and distractions bother you. Be equanimous. All novice meditators will pass through this phase during their early meditation practice. They find the mind wandering and not remaining fixed on the object of meditation, which in this case is the breath. The mind is like the proverbial attention-deficit monkey who can rarely stay still for more than a few seconds. He will jump from one branch of a tree to another all the time, in spite of the fact that the branch on which he sits is full of luscious tender leaves and edible ripe fruits. He is constantly on the lookout for 'greener pastures'. There are several well-known ways out of this conundrum. The first is the counting method. A novice will start counting the breath when he notices that the mind is wandering, but he does so only up to ten.[2] If the mind continues to wander he will repeat this exercise as many times as is necessary for him again to focus exclusively on the breath.

The second method is to 'label' all distractions as soon

as they appear by identifying each distraction with just a single word. For example, 'car', 'TV', 'dog', 'thinking' and so on, and then letting go of the distraction and getting back to mindful meditation on the breath.

vii. Having got rid of distractions and having learnt to keep the mind from wandering, it is *wordless* observation of the breath.

viii. *Vipassanā* meditation is an active function. It is awareness through one-pointedness.

ix. As your concentration deepens, you will have less trouble with an agitated mind.

x. Your breathing will now slow down and you will be able to follow it more and more clearly with fewer interruptions. You will begin to experience a state of great calm in which you enjoy complete freedom from physical irritants such as greed, lust, envy, jealousy and hatred. These are beautiful, clear, blissful states of the mind.

xi. These blissful states are, however, temporary and will end when the meditation session ends.

However, in spite of all our efforts there is a class of hindrances that can affect our progress. These are called *nīvaraṇa*. For instance, we may experience impatience with lack of progress, or aversion in the form of anger, or depression because progress seems slow. Sometimes lethargy overwhelms us, and we doze off as soon as we start to meditate. Sometimes we may be so agitated that we fidget or find excuses to avoid meditating. At other times scepticism undermines the will to continue, unreasoning doubts about the methodology or about your teacher, or even about our own ability to meditate.

At such moments we must understand that these hindrances have arisen only in reaction to our success in practising mindfulness with clear comprehension (*sati-sampajañña*)[1]. If we persevere, they are bound to disappear gradually.

The five *nīvaraṇas* (hindrances) really are all in the mind. They are:

1. Sensual desire
2. Aversion or anger, ill will and hatred
3. Sloth and torpor or lethargy, which simply is mental laziness.
4. Agitation (restlessness)
5. Doubt.

We must remember that all the five hindrances are mental factors. They are not self, just impersonal factors functioning in their own way.

In the *suttas* we find a simile illustrating the effect of these different obstructions. Imagine a pond of clear water where a rare gem lies at the bottom. We now add a number of bright dyes to the water, which then takes on beautiful psychedelic patterns. We become entranced with the beauty and intricacy of the colours and do not penetrate to the depths. This can be compared to sensual desires. Anger, ill will and aversion can be compared to boiling water. Water that is boiling, as in a geyser, is very turbulent and we cannot see through to the bottom. Sloth and torpor are like the pond getting covered by a dense layer of algae. One cannot possibly penetrate to the bottom. Restlessness and worry are like a wind-swept pond. The surface is agitated and the bottom is impenetrable. Doubt is like the water when muddied; the bottom is obscured.

Now how can we deal with these enemies?

Happily, there are specific ways to deal with them as they confront us along the path. The first is to recognize them, to see them clearly every moment they appear. This very recognition is the most powerful and effective way of overcoming them. Recognition leads to mindfulness and mindfulness means not clinging, not condemning and not identifying oneself with the object. All hindrances are impermanent mental factors. They arise and pass away. If we are mindful of them as soon as they arise, do only note them without reacting, (in fact, decline to identify ourselves with them); then they would pass through the mind without creating 'waves'. Mindfulness is the best and most effective way of dealing with them.

We can then see the bottom of the pond clearly and we will find no difficulty in picking up this rare gem, which as you already would have guessed, is 'wisdom'. As we know, this wisdom leads to insight and insight in turn leads to liberation.

Three steps in *Vipassanā* meditation

Once a novice meditator has learnt to concentrate on the breath, or any other subject of his choice for a reasonable period of time and to stay focused, he is ready to be introduced to insight or *vipassanā* meditation proper. *Vipassanā* or insight is the experiential understanding of the real nature of all phenomena in one's own mind and body. It is the very same model, which the Buddha adopted on the day of his Enlightenment. It is to observe with a clear unclouded and non-judgmental mind each and every thing happening in this fathom-long body.

We need to follow this same method and observe and develop insight within ourselves experientially. The universal method of insight meditation consists of a three-fold, graduated course corresponding to three stages of insight development.[2]

Step 1 - Walking meditation

The meditator will choose a subject such as the breath, or walking, to discriminate mentally and recognize the subtle differences in the ultimate constituents of actuality *via* the chosen subject of meditation. Let us assume that he has selected walking meditation.

In *vipassanā* meditation, a crucial factor is learning to concentrate and to be mindful. You will remember that previously, we learnt to concentrate and be mindful of the breath while in the sitting posture. Walking meditation too can lead to concentration as well as awareness. With proper walking meditation one can even gain insight into mind and matter and their impermanence.

A meditator should practise walking meditation with full awareness of the manner in which the steps are taken. At this introductory stage, he should note as 'left' when he takes a left step and when taking a right step, to note it as 'right'. The mind must observe the movement of the foot. He should lay stress on awareness, sharp awareness of the movement of the foot. To do walking meditation, he will need a private place with enough space for about eight or more paces. He will be walking back and forth very slowly.

The physical directions for walking meditation proper are simple. Start at one end and stay for the time it takes to breathe two or three times. Your arms should be held in a way that is comfortable in front, behind or at your sides. Lift the heel of one foot, then rest that foot on its toes. Next lift the foot and carry it forward slowly in a short step and then bring it down. Next shift your weight onto this leg and then slowly repeat with the other foot. Continue till you come to the end of the walk and stop for the time it takes you to breathe twice. About-turn clockwise, very slowly and mindfully, (this is in keeping with the Buddhist tradition of circumambulation). On completion of the turn, remain stationary for two breaths, then proceed walking in the previous fashion till you come back to your starting point. Repeat this slow walking with mindfulness and total concentration until it is time to end your meditation session. Remember to keep your head up and your neck relaxed. Keep your eyes open to maintain balance, but in a rather unfocussed manner so that you are not looking at anything in particular. Walk naturally but at the slowest pace that is comfortable. Watchout for tensions as soon as you spot them. Your objective is to attain total alertness, heightened sensitivity and a full, unblocked experience of the motion of walking.

You will now observe that a step, which appeared to be

smooth and continuous, is in fact composed of a complex series of tiny activities. Try not to miss anything. You can break down each step to many component parts. At the start you can notice at least four of these: lifting of the foot, moving the foot forward, dropping it down and shifting the body weight onto that foot.

You will also see that with good concentration you will not be aware of the form of the foot. Nor will you be aware of the body or bodily form. What you know is just movement of the foot. You will in fact find yourself fully immersed in a fluid, unbroken awareness of motion.

If your mind wanders, note the distraction in the usual way, then return your attention to walking. **Don't think, just feel. Register the sensations as they flow**. The *vipassanā* walking technique is designed to flood your consciousness with simple sensations, and to do it so thoroughly that all else is pushed aside. When you do so over a period of time, many things are revealed to you.

Let us discuss the practice of walking meditation a little more. We started by trying to be mindful of the act of stepping, then we moved onto focusing on two stages of walking. Stepping and putting the foot down, stepping, putting down. We then started to note mindfully four stages in each step. Raising our heel, lifting our foot, moving it forward and finally placing it on the ground. We progressed to the point where we noted five stages: Raising, lifting, moving, placing (frequently called 'pressing'), and shifting your weight.

By now you should have realized that when you were mindful of these five stages when taking a single step, you were naturally slowing down your walking, which came automatically. This slowing down is particularly beneficial because it is only then that you can be truly mindful and fully aware of all the movements. Whereas previously you thought that when taking a step it was a continuous movement, you now realize that this is not so. The raising movement of the heel is not mixed with the lifting movement of the foot and the lifting movement of the foot is not mixed with the moving forward movement, and so on. You will observe all movements clearly and distinctly.

As *vipassanā* meditators, you will notice much more as you continue with the practice. When you lift the foot you will experience the lightness of the foot. When you push the foot forward you will notice movement from one place to another. When you put the foot down you will feel the heaviness of the foot because the foot becomes heavier and heavier as it descends. When you put the foot down and shift your weight, you feel the touch of the ground as either hard or soft.

When you observe these four processes you are perceiving the four primary particles - they are the solid, liquid, heat/caloricity and finally air particles.

Let us go into a little more detail about the characteristics of these primary elements during walking meditation. In the first movement of lifting the foot when you felt lightness, you perceived caloricity. This energy allows us to raise the foot and move it forward, but in the lifting and carrying forward of the foot there was also movement. Movement is one aspect of air and it is dominant as we move the foot forward. When you move the foot down, there is a kind of heaviness in the foot. Heaviness is a characteristic of liquid.

Thus you have perceived the liquid element. Finally when pressing the foot down and shifting your weight onto that foot, you perceive the hardness or softness of the ground. You have now felt the characteristic and the nature of solidity and have seen, experientially, the composition of the aggregates of *rūpa* or matter.

We thus see that in just one step, we can perceive many processes. Only those who practise walking meditation can ever hope to see these things.

When you continue to practise walking meditation you will come to realize that with every movement, there is also the noting mind, the awareness of movement. There is the lifting movement and the awareness of the lifting movement, then the movement and the awareness thereof, and so on. You then come to realize that both the movement and the mind (which is aware of the movement) arise and disappear in that very moment. Movement — awareness-disappearance. The moment of awareness is in the mind, whereas matter achieves the movement of the foot. In other words, mentality and materiality are working together.

Another thing, which you discovered, is that an intention precedes every one of the movements. You lift your foot because you want to. You move it forward because you want to, and so on. You thus realize that an intention has always preceded a movement, and you understood from practical experience that, as the Buddha said, "mind is the forerunner of all phenomena". This discovery by actual experience and practice during *vipassanā* meditation is the first of the *vipassanā* insights. It is called *nāma-rūpa-pariccheda-ñāṇa*, or insight knowledge of how mind and matter always work together.

You now understand that there is a cause or a condition for every movement, and in this case, the condition is the intention preceding each movement. You thus finally comprehend the relationship of conditioning and the conditioned, cause and effect. With this understanding, you have taken a giant step forward in your meditation.

Meditation on the Breath

If you have selected the breath as the preferred subject for meditation, you will begin the practice as outlined in the foregoing pages. You will, instead of letting go of disturbances and thoughts, address them with equanimity as they appear, and only let them go after contemplation and realizing that they are nothing but phenomena which arise, stay awhile and then pass away. *(uppāda, ṭhiti, bhaṅga)*. You will also realize that they are at the fundamental level, void or empty of a permanent core.

Taking stock

We are now well on our way: a voyage within our own body and mind to find the truth unclouded by the delusion of a self-perpetuating 'I'. However, before we proceed to the next step in *vipassanā* meditation, it is useful to take stock of how far we have progressed in the development of the mind, for we need to make sure that we have removed all negative feelings and emotions which would otherwise impede our progress. If we continue to harbour hatred, aversion, greed, selfishness and sensual desires, it will virtually be impossible for us to proceed towards the development of insight.

There are many known methods for getting rid of these negativities permanently. One proven method is for us to look inwards during a meditation session and see with an open, non-judgmental mind whether we indeed have these negative characteristics within ourselves or not. Another recommended way is to contemplate on the opposite positive factors, namely the four sublime states or *brahma-vihāras* of universal kindness, compassion, participating joy and equanimity. When we do so, taking one subject at a time, we can see whether even the tiniest of their opposites are yet in our minds or not.

The Buddha has laid down a method for developing the sublime states: "Here, monks, a disciple dwells pervading one direction with his heart filled with loving-kindness, likewise the second, the third and the fourth direction; so above, below and around; he dwells pervading the entire world everywhere and equally with his heart filled with loving-kindness, abundant, grown great, measureless, free from enmity and free of distress." (D.13). He repeats the same advice for the other three sublime states as well. We need only replace the word loving-kindness with either compassion or participating joy or equanimity.

In 'pervading' and 'directions', one's thoughts should be directed first to the east, then to the west, next to the north and then to the south. This should be followed by directing one's thoughts to the areas in between and finally to the zenith and the nadir, i.e., above and below, including the skies and birds and the seas and fish and so on.

In practising meditation using loving-kindness as a model, we first repeat the 'invocation' or 'wish' as given earlier and then we direct such thoughts to those we love, and so on (as described in the invocation) till we come to disagreeable people. This of course is the hardest task, but as true meditators we can breakdown the remaining barriers by heroic effort. We make no discriminations in our pervasive thoughts of loving-kindness, and extend our thoughts of loving-kindness equally to all. (There is a Sinhala saying which comes to mind: "when serving rice, do so to everyone using the very same spoon")[3].

At this point of proper practice, we should have come to a higher stage of concentration, and we would in fact have reached access-concentration (*upacāra-samādhi*). Further progress will lead to full concentration (*appanā*) reaching fruition as the first *jhāna,* then onto the higher *jhānas.* The ultimate aim of attaining the *jhānas* relating to the four sublime states is to produce a state of mind that can serve as a firm foundation for the development of liberating insight into the true nature of all phenomena as being impermanent, subject to suffering and being void. A mind that has achieved meditational absorption induced by the *Brahma-vihāra* (sublime states) will now be pure, tranquil, firm, collected and largely free of negativities. A meditator is then well prepared for the final effort, which is aimed at deliverance.

Meditative development of the sublime states will be aided by repeated reflection upon the benefits they bring and the dangers of their opposites. As the Buddha has said 'What a person considers and reflects upon for a long time, to that his mind will bend and incline'[5].

Step 2 of *vipassanā* meditation

As persons who have made a study of the *paṭiccasamuppāda* in the previous chapters, it would be appropriate to use it as the subject for our advanced *vipassanā* meditation. This is also particularly appropriate because of the fact that the Buddha on his road to enlightenment used this very subject for His awakening. The Buddha categorically says that this was His eye-opening discovery in one sentence: 'He who sees Dependent Origination sees the Dhamma. He who sees the Dhamma sees Dependent Origination (M. 28) . Arahat Assaji was the first to see this clearly, as was shown earlier.

Meditating on the *Paṭiccasamuppāda*.

The meditator will now look at the *paṭiccasamuppāda* as part of his personal experience from different angles. He contemplates, reflects and analyzes it. He finds that whichever way he looks at it, the inevitable conclusion in the ultimate sense is that there is no being or individual, but only a continuity of conditioned, dependent phenomena occurring in what appears as a causal chain constantly undergoing origination and dissolution.

With further application of concentration focused into laser-sharpness, he looks again at the twelve links of the *paṭiccasamuppāda* in the forward and reverse directions. Forward contemplation shows us the existence of suffering. He first sees how ignorance sets in motion the life cycle. Ignorance thus conditions action, and action conditions consciousness. From consciousness he proceeds to contemplation of name-and-form, then the six senses and so on. Finally he sees that craving leads to clinging and then to becoming. With becoming he sees that birth is inevitable. Now with insight he sees that birth is always followed by sickness, ageing and death - all of which cause considerable suffering. Contemplating the twelve links in this manner will lead him to a profound understanding of mind-matter phenomena called an individual (*puggala*).

He would then practise the reverse contemplation, but he should not do so by starting with the twelfth link and proceeding backwards to the first link. On the contrary, he should start in this case too with ignorance, for, once there is no ignorance, there will be no deluded action. When actions are not governed by greed, hatred and delusion, he sees that there is no defilement of consciousness. He proceeds in this manner till he comes to becoming, birth and death — thus seeing with insight how this whole chain of becoming ceases. He then realizes that he has been gradually engaging the Eight-fold Path (the Fourth Noble Truth) of skilful understanding, skilful thought, skilful action and so on, to put an end to the chain of suffering.

He next sees that this five-aggregate 'person' is at the ultimate level nothing but a combination of the five formations or the five groups of clinging (*pañcupadānakkhandha*) which are subject to decay, suffering and death. He also sees with insight that he cannot find a permanent core or entity in the entire conditioned dependent chain. He finds only phenomena and becomes detached from them, and with this detachment he comprehends the fact of non-self or *anatta*.

The meditator now spreads his focus to other phenomena and sees clearly that all formations, which he looks at, along with their causes and conditions, originate and dissolve before his very eyes. They are all impermanent, *anicca*.

At this point of self-realization, a meditator is often beset by certain corruptions of insight called *vipassanā upakkilesa*. These are extraordinary experiences that arise when insight meditation begins to gather momentum. Examples are the perception of one or more of the following: bright lights, an aura around the meditator, a sharp increase in understanding, happiness, rapture, or a feeling of being energized. While these are useful indicators telling the meditator that he is now progressing well, they become corruptions or *kilesa* when he begins to get attached and proceeds to enjoy and dwell in them, thinking that he is now liberated.

The meditator should instead, recognize them merely as imposters and examine these experiences with equanimity and according to the three universal characteristics of all conditioned phenomena, namely as impermanent, subject to suffering and non-self. With this insight he will then let go and proceed with renewed enthusiasm.

In the second stage of insight meditation we have used the subject of *paṭiccasamuppāda* because of our familiarity with it. There are, in addition, numerous topics that are suitable for advanced meditation. In fact, in the *Mahā Satipaṭṭhāna Sutta* itself, the Buddha has recommended four subjects as suitable for insight meditation, which are:

> The Body (including the breath) - *kāyānupassanā*
> Feelings or sensations - *vedanānupassanā*
> The mind - *cittānupassanā* and
> Mental formations- *dhammānupassanā*.

Out of all of these, the breath often takes precedence as the subject most suitable for meditation. However, it is the meditation teacher who will be the most competent person to suggest a meditation subject to the novice meditator, and he will do so according to his assessment of the novice's individual aptitudes.

Step 3 in *vipassanā* meditation

The meditator who has practised insight meditation successfully at stage two for some time, will now continue self-examination with added zest and energy. He will observe non-judgmentally everything happening within his body, while at the same time not allowing proliferation of thoughts. He will merely observe phenomena: their appearance, short existence and immediate dissolution (*uppāda, ṭhiti, bhaṅga*), unconnected to anything else.

He will then be following the instructions that the Buddha gave the advanced meditator, Bāhiya Dārucīriya – an injunction so deep that it brought Bāhiya to enlightenment right on the spot:

"In the seen there will be only the seen; in the heard there will be only the heard; in the sensed there will be only the sensed; in the cognized there will be only the cognized. This is how you must train yourself, Bāhiya" (*Udāna*,1:10).

The meditator now sees with insight that all formations within himself, as well as in the whole universe, are indeed characterized by impermanence, unsatisfactoriness and devoid of 'self'. (see foot-note 5). He fixes his mind on just one of the above characteristics and quite soon is able to make a break-through to full understanding. Noble Path-consciousness arises, and he transcends the mundane and passes to the supramundane, which is the peace of Nibbāna, for the first time.

On the other hand, if he is contemplating and reflecting on the *paṭiccasamuppāda*, he would be fixing his mind on all three characteristics simultaneously, and it will not be long before he too is able, as in the previous example, to transcend the mundane, pass onto the supramundane peace of Nibbāna for the first time. He then completes the experiential understanding of the Four Noble Truths by attaining the knowledge of the Path of stream entry, *sotāpatti-magga-ñāṇa*. He has totally uprooted and discarded forever the three fetters, the of false view of personality, doubt and attachment to rites and rituals.

He rounds up his effort by achieving the knowledge of fruition (*phala-ñāṇa*) and the blissful peace of Nibbāna. It is at this stage that there arises in the meditator the reviewing knowledge of the Path and the Fruit (table 5.2. *item* 16) by which the meditator reviews the defilements that have been eliminated and those that yet remain.

A noble disciple may perhaps not stop now. What is left is only the need to eliminate the remaining seven defilements or fetters in order to become an Arahat - the fully liberated person.

Chapter VII

Concluding Remarks

We have now completed our journey of discovery, for we have explored the 'world', – our body and mind in the light of the Dhamma.

The Buddha has shown that the first critical step on our way to liberation is to first understand and comprehend the doctrine of dependent origination: "It is through not understanding, not penetrating this doctrine that this generation has become entangled like a tangled ball of string unable to pass beyond the round of *saṁsāra*." (M.ii.55). The final step is to practise the Dhamma *via* the Four Noble Truths, for we now realize that liberation is not possible until we eradicate ignorance (*avijjā*) and the three root defilements of greed (*loba*), hatred (*dosa*) and delusion (*moha*) by following the Noble Eightfold Path, and *vipassanā* meditation.

When we do so, it can be as rewarding an experience for you, as it has been for me. We would perhaps have also realized that *vipassanā* meditation when targeted towards liberation entails an intensive and dedicated practice, for:

> "The heights by great men reached and kept
> Were not attained by sudden flight,
> But they, while their companions slept,
> Were toiling upward in the night." Longfellow 1807-82.

Nevertheless, a meditator should not over-strain himself whilst meditating. Here the importance of equanimity must be stressed. The meditator will then realize that meditation can be a pleasant and rewarding experience. This is why members of the *Ariya Saṅgha* – The Noble Ones, all had smiling faces.

When we 'live' the Dhamma in all of our waking hours, we will in effect be meditating, reflecting in the proper way *yoniso-manasikāra* and contemplating with total awareness and mindfulness all the time. It is with this paradigm shift, that meditation, like one's breath, becomes 'second nature' to us.

Insight and the development of understanding come when the mind is quiet. When we have an open and non-judgmental mind and see everything happening in our own body and mind from moment to moment with insight, the true Dhamma unwinds before our very eyes, and we commence to see the truth. How fast we progress thereafter depends solely on our individual efforts and abilities.

Let us not regret the past but let go of it and remember that we have the rest of our lives to achieve liberation.

> "A fellow went to a Zen master and said, If I work very
>   hard, how soon can I be enlightened?
> The Zen master looked him up and down and said,' ten
>   years'.
> The fellow said, 'No, listen, I mean if I really worked
>   hard at it, how long --'
> The Zen master cut him off 'I am sorry I misjudged,
>   twenty years'
> 'What!' said the young man, "You don't understand!
>   I'm...'

'Thirty years,' said the Zen master.
From 'Buddhism Plain and Simple' by Steve Hagen.

This brings us to the end of the presentation. It is the hope and fervent wish of the author that readers benefit from its perusal, which, for maximum benefit, should be accompanied by earnest contemplation, reflection, meditation and last but not least, genuine dedicated application.

May All Beings Develop Insight and Realize Liberation!

Bibliography (sequential)

1. Piyadassi Mahathera, The Spectrum of Buddhism, 1991, ISBN 0-955-9098-03-9.
2. Bhikkhu Bodhi, The Buddha and His Dhamma, 1999, ISBN 0-955-24-0201-8.
3. Narada Mahathera, The Buddha and His Teachings, 1997, BPS. Kandy, Sri Lanka.
4. Walpola Rahula Mahathera, What the Buddha Taught, 1959, ISBN 0-8021-303-3.
5. Ron Wijewantha, The Life and Message of the Buddha, 1990, Limited Edition.
6. The Dalai Lama, A flash of Lightning, ISBN 0-87773-971-4.
7. K.N.Jayatilleke, The Message of the Buddha, 1979, Limited Edition.
8. Bhikkhu Bodhi, A Comprehensive Manual of

Abhidhamma, 1999, ISBN 0-955-24-0198-4.

9. Peter Della Santina, The Tree of Enlightenment, 1997, EN099-1335, (Printed and published by the Corporate Body of the Buddha Educational Foundation) Taipei. Taiwan.

10. Tanissaro Bhikkhu, The Wings of Awakening, (An anthology of the Pali Canon), 1996 EN 115-1640-. (Printed and distributed by the Corporate Body of the Buddhist Educational Foundation), Taipei, Taiwan.

11 Bhikkhu Bodhi, Transcendental dependent origination, 1980, ISSN, 0049-7541.

12. John Walters, Mind Unshaken, ISBN, 0-955-9219-75-8.

13. Bhikkhu Bodhi, The Great Discourse on Causation, 1995, BP211S, BPS, Kandy, Sri Lanka.

14. Mahasi Sayadaw, Practical Insight Meditation, ISBN 955-24-0089-9.

15. Nyanatiloka, Buddhist Dictionary, 1980, BPS, Kandy, Sri Lanka.

16. Ñāṇārama Mahathera, The Seven Contemplations of Insight, 1997, BPS, ISBN 95524-0124-0.

Other Recommended Reading

1. Piyadassi Mahathera, Dependent Origination, ISBN 0-955-24-0172-0.

2. U. Pandita, In This Very Life, 1992, ISBN, 0-955-24-0094-5.

3. Bhikkhu Bodhi, The Noble Eightfold Path, 1994, ISBN 0-955-24-0116-0.

4 Bhadantacariya Buddhaghosa, The Visuddhimagga, The Path of Purification, Translated by Bhikkhu Nanamoli. BPS. 1991.

Books on Vipassanā Meditation

1. Practical Insight Meditation, (Basic and Progressive Stages), Mahasi Sayadaw, 1991, BPS, Sri Lanka, ISBN 955-24-0089-0.

2. The Progress of Insight, Mahasi Sayadaw, 1994, BPS, Sri Lanka, ISBN, 955-24-0090-2.

3. The Art Of Living, (Vipassanā meditation), William Hart, (As taught by S.N.Goenka), 1987, Harper Row, ISBN 0-06-063724-2.

4. Mahā Satipaṭṭhāna Suttam, 1993, (Goenka translation), Vipassana Research Publication, Dharmagiri, Igatapuri, Maha Rashtra, India.

5. In This Very Life, U Pandita, 1992, Wisdom, ISBN 955-24-0094-5.

6. Mindfulness (In Plain English), Henepola Gunaratana Mahathera, 1991, Wisdom, ISBN 0-86171-064-9.

7. The Four Foundations of Mindfulness, U.Silananda, 1990, Wisdom, ISBN. 0-86171-092-4.

Some Vipassanā Meditation Centers and Retreats in the U.S.A.

Chico Dharma Study Foundation, Director, Peter D. Santina, 26 Kirkway, Chico, CA 95928.

Metta Forest Monastery, Director, Ven Thanissaro Bhikkhu, P.O.Box 1409, Valley Center, CA 92082.

Vipassana Meditation Center. (Goenka), P.O.Box 24, Shelbourne Falls, MA 01370.

Bhavana Society, Director, Ven Henepola Gunaratana, Route 1, Box 218-3, High View, WV 26808.

Spirit Rock Meditation Center, P.O.Box 169, Woodacre, CA 94973.

Abhayagiri Buddhist Monastery 16201, Tomki Road, Redwood Valley, CA 05470.

* * * * * * * * * *

Some Texts containing material on the
Paṭiccasamuppāda

1. Visuddhimagga-*Path of Purification,* Chapter 17, Trans. Bhikkhu Nanamoli.
2. Paṭisambhidāmagga, (PTS).
3. Paṭisambhidamagga Aṭṭhakathā (Sinhala script, Simon Hewavitarana Bequest).
3. Sutta pitaka, (PTS).
4. The Sālistamba Sutra, N.Ross Reat, Motilal Banasidass Publishers Pvt.Delhi.
5. Paṭṭhāna of the Abhidhamma Piṭaka.
6. The Wings of Awakening, Tanissaro Bhikkhu, 1999, Corporate Body of the Buddhist Educational Foundation, Taipei, Taiwan, R.O.C.s
7. The Tree of Enlightenment, Peter D.Santina, 1998, Corporate Body of the Buddhist Educational Foundation, Taipei, Taiwan, R.O.C.
8. Mahā Nidāna Sutta, The Great Discourse on Causation and its Commentaries, Translation plus a long introductory essay, Bhikkhu Bodhi, BPS. 1984.

* * * * * * * * * *

Footnotes

CHAPTER I

1. *Paṭiccasamuppāda*: (Sanskrit: *Pratītyasamutpāda*) – dependent origination; the twelve-factor cyclical process of causal conditioning affecting the perpetuation of *saṁsāric* existence which must be broken or transcended in order to make progress on the spiritual path to Nibbāna.

2. **Four Noble Truths**. See pp.5ff.

3. **Vipassanā (*bhāvanā*)**: the systematic development of insight through the meditation method of observing the reality of oneself by observing sensations (feelings) within one's own body.

4. **Dhamma:** the teachings of the Buddha.

5. **Sangha:** the community of Buddhist monks and nuns.

6. **Piyadassi Thera,** Spectrum of Buddhism, 1991.

7. **Bikkhu Bodhi,** The Buddha and His Dhamma, 1999.

8. **Enlightenment:** 'awakening', achievement of supreme knowledge, and liberation. The enlightenment of a Buddha is called *sammā-sambodhi*- 'perfect Enlightenment'.

9. **Nibbāna:** (Sanskrit – *Nirvāṇa*): extinction, the ultimate reality, the unconditioned.

10. **Wijewantha Ron,** *The Life and Message of the Buddha*, 1990.

11. **Kamma**: Action, specifically an action performed by oneself that will have a repercussion in one's future.

12. **Bhikkhu Bodhi,** *The Noble Eightfold Path*, (B.P.S), 1994.

13. *Saṁsāra*: the conditioned; it is the round of existence of rebirths which is transcended with the realization of enlightenment.

14. **Deity** *(deva)*: a heavenly being.

15. **Insight**: is the intuitive exposing of the truth of impermanency, suffering and impersonal nature of all corporeal and mental phenomena of existence. It is by *vipassanā* meditation that this *vipassanā-paññā* (insight-wisdom) is developed and revealed.

16. **Dalai Lama,** A Flash of Lightning in the Dark, 1994.

17. **Transcendental/Supramundane:** That which is beyond even the concept of reality, – that which transcends all thoughts.

****

CHAPTER II

1. **Kuru.** The people inhabiting a market town called Kammāssadhamma.

2. **Mahā Satipaṭṭhāna Sutta.** A discourse on the four-fold mindfulness, containing detailed instructions on insight meditation and the assurance that following and

  practising the instructions will lead to liberation from suffering

3. **Suttas**. The discourses of the Buddha.

4. **Supra-mundane:transcendental** *(lokuttara)*. This is a term for the 4 paths and fruits of *sotāpanna, sakadāgāmi, anāgāmi and arahat*. As opposed to this is 'mundane, *(lokiya)*', which refers to all states of consciousness arising in the 'worldling'. Mundane thoughts can also arise in the Noble Ones but not *vice-versa*. When mundane thoughts arise in the Noble Ones such thoughts are not associated with the supra-mundane paths and fruition. (Nyanatiloka, Buddhist Dictionary).

5. **Abhidhamma-piṭaka**. The third 'basket' or 'piṭaka' comprising the collection of higher teachings, i.e. the systematic philosophical exegesis of the Dhamma (the Buddha's doctrine). The first 'piṭaka' or basket is the Sutta *piṭaka* (the collection of the discourses of the Buddha); the second *piṭaka* or 'basket' is the Vinaya-*piṭaka* (rules of discipline for monks and nuns). The name given to all three of the above is 'Tripiṭaka' — literally, "' three baskets".

6. **Manual of Abhidhamma**, 1999, Editor, Bhikkhu Bodhi.

7. *Ibid.*

8. **H.Gunaratana MahaThera**. A personal communication.

* For an elegant, simple essay on this subject, read "The selfmade private prison" by Prof Lily de Silva, BPS, Bodhi Leaves, No.120.

Chapter III

1. **Devas** – see ch1. f.n.14

2. *Pratītya-samutpāda* – The Sanskrit spelling of the Pāli word *paṭiccasamuppāda* as it appears in Mahāyāna sūtras

3. **Tripiṭaka.** Literally, "three baskets" or collections of the teachings of the Buddha, namely: 1. The Sutta-piṭaka — the collection of discourses, (2). The Vinaya-piṭaka - the collection of monastic rules for Buddhist monks and nuns. And 3. The Abhidhamma-piṭaka - the collection of higher teachings or philosophical exegesis of the Dhamma.

4. **Nibbāna:** see ch1. fn9.

5. **Paccaya**: The 24 conditions. 'Condition' is something on which something else, the so-called 'conditioned thing' is dependent, and without which the latter cannot be. For a full explanation and table of the 24 modes of conditionality, see "Buddhist Dictionary" by Nyanatiloka, BPS, 1990.

6. Later, Arahat Sāriputta.

(** Alternately you can replace 'from' with 'dependent on' and 'comes' with 'arises').

CHAPTER IV

1. *Gandhabba*. Often thought to be the rebirth-linking or very first consciousness of the being to be born.
2. Thanissaro Bhikkhu, *The Wings of Awakening*. 1996.
3. Piyadassi Mahathera, *The Spectrum of Buddhism*.

****

CHAPTER V

1. *Transcendental Dependant Origination* — Bhikkhu Bodhi, Wheel Publication Nos. 277/278. BPS, Kandy, Sri Lanka.
2. *Sutta-piṭaka* The discourses of the Buddha as contained in the *Tripiṭaka*.
3. Mahasi Sayadaw a. *Practical Insight Meditation,* B.P.S. 1991.
4. Ñāṇārāma Mahathera, *The Seven Contemplations of Insight* B.P S, 1997.
5. *Visuddhimagga, The Path of Purification*, Translated by Bhikkhu Nanamoli, 1993 Ed.
6. *Paṭisambhidāmagga*, (PTS).

****

Future is not actually in our hands.

CHAPTER VI

1. *Sati-sampajañña* – *sati* is mindfulness, and *sampajañña* is thorough understanding or comprehension, the two together, *sati-sampajañña* is defined as 'mindfulness with clear comprehension.'

2. The counting method has several variations depending on the teacher.

3. Sinhala- The main race and language of Sri Lanka.

4. *The Significance of dependent origination,* Nyanatiloka Mahathera, 1969.

5. The descriptions from this point onwards are theoretical and not based on personal experience of people I know.

****

Best part of the life is ahead ō us
I'll never be there alone,
you will be there c̄ me.

Bhavatu Sabba Mangalam
(May there be) Success in all endeavours.

About the Author

Ron Wijewantha was born in Sri Lanka in 1925. He received his BSc. (Hons.) degree and his Master's degree from the London University. The University of California awarded him the PhD degree in 1963. He now lives in retirement in California after a long and distinguished career in Sri Lanka's State Services.

Dr Wijewantha is a devout Buddhist and was ordained a member of the Sangha for a short period. He now spends most of his time in study of the Dhamma and in practising *vipassanā* meditation. He is also a *vipassanā* meditation teacher, and author of "The Life and Message of the Buddha - (A Book for Young People)."

handsome, young prince
felt the flame o love quicken in her heart
mystery unraveled